LIFE
BEFORE
DEATH

Praise for *Life Before Death*

Engaging, smart, persuasive, conversational, and full of stories—Ian's book is just like Ian. Enjoy!

—Jerry B. Jenkins
Novelist

Ian Leitch is a wonderful servant of God. Having known Mr. Leitch for more than 30 years, I have seen firsthand his impeccable character. I have been blessed by his knowledge of the Bible, his anointed teaching and preaching, and his great sense of humor. I have the utmost respect for Mr. Leitch, and know full well that this book will impact countless lives.

—Luis Palau
Evangelist, Luis Palau Association

To know what happens when we are saved, we need to know what happened to Adam when he fell. Salvation is an exact reversal of Adam's fall. Ian Leitch explains that our problem is not that we are guilty, but that we are dead—spiritually dead. So the answer is much more than forgiveness: it is to receive Life, which is the only thing that counters death! And this life is the life of Christ Himself, who comes to live His life in us in order to express Himself through us. No wonder this book makes the Christian life possible, purposeful, and exciting!

—Charles Price, Sr.
Pastor, The Peoples Church, Toronto

Ian's book is relevant to the contemporary Christian, not merely as a decoration on the library shelves, but in active application in the believer's daily life. Life Before Death *is a trustworthy map for the home-hungry soul lost in the wilderness of detours, dead ends, and misdirection. For the believer peacefully at home in the practice of faith, this book is documentary evidence that standing firm on that which he knows is proper positioning for the celebration of grace.*

— JEANNETTE CLIFT GEORGE
Actress, author, founder and artistic
director of the A.D. Players

In my travels, I have been privileged to hear the finest Christian preachers and theologians of the past 40 years. I know of no one who so clearly, logically, and spiritually delineates the gospel of Jesus Christ as does Ian Leitch. Every time I hear him speak, I am refreshed again by the profound simplicity of the person and message of Christ. This book is just a sampling of Ian's exceptional gift for delivering that profound simplicity. Read it and discover again the wonder and life-changing power of the "simple gospel."

— JOHN HALL
Gospel singer, preacher,
Gospel-Net, Inc.

I have held Ian Leitch in the highest regard for the last 35 years. It is an honor to count him as my friend. Here in Scotland he has made a major impact over six decades through his preaching and teaching. Countless people have been won for the Kingdom of God as a result of his ministry, and thousands have grown in their faith through his stimulating teaching and seminars. His sensitivity to people, his wicked sense of humour, his culturally astute antennae, and his deep love for God's Word have been his hallmark and mirror the emphasis of the book he has written.

My own walk with God was powerfully influenced by Ian's simple yet profound explanations of the truths of the Gospel plus his emphasis on a disciplined study of God's Word and how to use practical systems to encourage my prayer life. He has been a real encouragement to my family, and his new book will undoubtedly be a rich blessing to all who read it.

— J. LORIMER GRAY
Executive director, Abernethy Trust

Ian Leitch can be summed up as "you get exactly what it says on the tin!"
He is passionate, full of integrity, a great communicator, a real evangelist,
and a fantastic friend! This book carries all the truths and passion that
Ian has consistently brought through his clear teaching ministry over
the years. We fully commend not only this book but also the man behind
the book!

— RAY AND NANCY GOUDIE
Directors of NGM (New Generation
Music and Mission), Bristol, UK

Ever long for a no-nonsense, bottom-line, easy-to-understand
explanation of the Christian message? Then read Life Before Death. *I've*
heard Ian proclaim this message on both sides of the Atlantic, in both
secular and church settings, over a period of four decades. Ian not only
knows how to articulate the gospel for seekers, his life commends it.

— DON SWEETING
Senior pastor, Cherry Creek
Presbyterian Church, Colorado

A simple, straightforward, no-nonsense presentation of the Christian
faith and discipleship. What makes this book so useful is that it comes
both from the pen and the heart of an internationally recognized
Christian leader whose ministry and experience over the years make
him effective. Its style reminds me of a comment attributed to the
Puritan era: I did preach what I did feel, what I did smartingly feel.
The best communicators always do!

— REV. DR. TONY SARGENT
International Christian College,
Glasgow, Scotland

Would you like to know the God of the universe? The good news is,
you can! Life Before Death *is a direct, forceful, gripping message about*
how you can know God through a life-changing relationship with Jesus
Christ. Ian Leitch cuts through any confusion and showcases what the
gospel of Jesus Christ is all about. It reads easy but runs deep. Here

is a book to be savored. If you read it with an open heart, your life could be changed forever. God truly does have a wonderful plan for your life, and this book makes that plan clear and compelling.

—DR. RAY PRITCHARD
President, Keep Believing Ministries
Author of *Stealth Attack, An Anchor for the Soul, The Healing Power of Forgiveness*

LIFE BEFORE DEATH

A Restored, Regenerated, and Renewed Life

Ian Leitch

Foreword by Joseph M. Stowell

Grace Acres Press
P.O. Box 22
Larkspur, CO 80118
888-700-GRACE (4722)
(303) 681-9995
(303) 681-9996 fax
CULTIVATING JOY   www.GraceAcresPress.com

Grace Acres Press also publishes books in a variety of electronic formats. Some content that appears in print may not be available in electronic books.

Unless otherwise noted, all Scripture quotations are taken from the HOLY BIBLE, NEW INTERNATIONAL VERSION.® Copyright © 1973, 1978, 1984 International Bible Society. Used by permission of Zondervan. All rights reserved. Available through www.biblegateway.com.

Library of Congress Cataloging-in-Publication Data:

Leitch, Ian, 1939–
   Life before death : a restored, regenerated, and renewed life / by
Ian Leitch.
      p.   cm.
   ISBN: 978-1-60265-007-7
      1. Apologetics.   I. Title.
BT1103.L45   2007
239— dc22   2007025896

Printed in Canada

10 09 08 07   01 02 03 04 05 06 07 08 09 10

I dedicate this book to my wife, Morag, who, early in our courtship (age 15!), said she would go anywhere, at any time, and at any cost to serve Jesus. She has and much more. Morag has been my best friend, critic, and encourager.

About the Author

IAN LEITCH

The Heralds Trust and Ian Leitch are familiar names in Christian circles, particularly in Scotland. Many still remember the group "The Heralds," who sang and presented the gospel in halls, cinemas, and theaters, and on television, during the 1950s, 1960s, and 1970s. An estimated 7,000 people became Christians through their ministry in these days. Ian was originally one of the vocalists with the group and also did the preaching.

Shortly after marrying his wife, Morag, in 1964, Ian went to the United States to study at Moody Bible Institute in 1966. After three years of study and pastoring Fairfield Avenue Baptist Church in Chicago, the Leitches returned to Scotland in the autumn of 1969, so that Ian could take up work as evangelist with The Heralds; The Heralds Trust was formed in 1970.

For the past thirty-eight years, Ian has been evangelist and Bible teacher with The Heralds Trust, traveling extensively in the United Kingdom, North America (more than 150 visits), Europe, Haiti, India, and Guatemala. Over the past thirty-two years, Ian has pioneered a traveling Bible school called the "New Life" seminars. These week-long seminars run Monday to Friday, each evening. More than 9,000 people have attended these seminars.

Ian has worked closely with Luis Palau, Moody Bible Institute, and Baptist Union of Scotland. He has spoken at Filey Convention, England; the Baptist General Conference youth, Wheaton, Illinois; Youth Convention, Fellowship Baptists of Canada, Niagara Falls; Baptist Youth World Conference; and many other conferences, including Moody Keswick, Florida; Maranatha, Michigan; Winona Lake, Indiana; Cannon Beach, Oregon; Muskoka Baptist Conference, Elim Lodge, and Fair Havens in Canada; and Spring Harvest, Scotland.

Another side of Ian's ministry has been teaching apologetics at Scottish Baptist College and Capernwray Bible Schools, as well as teaching the New Life seminars in Albania, India, and Romania.

Ian has developed "Each One Bring One" evangelism based on meals from breakfasts to suppers. You cannot attend if you do not bring a non-Christian. Ian is the after-meal speaker. Thousands have come to Christ through these events.

Ian's unique personality and pulpit style appeal to people of all ages, and his enthusiasm for the gospel and godliness are contagious. He is committed to the inerrancy of Scripture: on that basis his faith is built and his work is determined. His heart is that of an evangelist. He is never happier than when he is presenting the gospel, whether in a cathedral, a university, a house group, or the open air.

In fact, over the years Ian has spoken at many schools, colleges, and universities in various countries.

Ian has long connections with his home church, Charlotte Baptist Chapel. His grandfather, Blacksmith Brown, was responsible for starting the open-air ministry in the chapel. His mother, Jessie Brown, was converted during the revival days of Rev. Joseph Kemp. His father, Arthur Leitch, and mother were married by Dr. Graham Scroggie; thereafter, his mother left the chapel to worship with her husband in the Christian Brethren.

Ian is the youngest of three brothers. Murray is in membership at Charlotte Chapel and Arthur is a retired pastor living in England.

Ian returned to his mother's church in his middle teens. He was leader of the Youth Ministry for three years and it was there that he met Morag MacLean. The MacLean family was also well known in the chapel, where Morag's mother played the piano on many occasions for soloists during Dr. Scroggie's ministry. Morag's father, Alexander MacLean, was a well-known and much-appreciated Baptist Union lay preacher. Ian and Morag were baptized by Dr. Gerald Griffiths and married by Dr. Alan Redpath. They left for America in 1966 with the blessing of the chapel. Upon their return, the Elders of Charlotte Chapel commissioned Ian to the ministry of The Heralds. Ian continues to have a close relationship with his church, its elders, and its pastor.

Ian and Morag celebrated 43 years of marriage in 2007. Their son, Steve, is married to Michaela; they have two daughters, Hope and Skye, and reside in South Carolina. Ian and Morag make their home in Balerno, Scotland.

Contents

Foreword

Getting our wayward lives into sync with God's good and productive ways can be a challenge. Thankfully, my friend Ian Leitch offers clear and helpful insights to help us live to the max and stay on track!

—JOSEPH M. STOWELL
Teaching Pastor,
Harvest Bible Chapel
Former President,
Moody Bible Institute

Acknowledgments

I gratefully acknowledge the following people, whose lives and words are found throughout this book.

My father lived the life of faith, which set the standard early in my life. It was a simple, observable faith I couldn't miss. It was a winsome faith that touched the lives that crossed his path. It was a working faith that I wanted for myself.

In my late teens, Alex Cameron came into my life. I was involved in the youth group at Charlotte Chapel in Edinburgh. Alex was the elder responsible for overseeing that youth group. His influence on my life, from open-air meetings to boys' camp to the beginning of The Heralds Gospel Group, was immeasurable and continues to this day.

Our pastor at that time, Dr. Alan Redpath, thundered the Victorious Christian Life from the pulpit Sunday after Sunday and challenged us to total commitment. This resulted in Morag and me flying to Chicago, where I attended Moody Bible Institute, and after graduation returning to the ministry of The Heralds Trust. Dr. Redpath was a friend and a role model.

In 1976, at the British Evangelists Conference, I listened to Major Ian Thomas present three messages that revolutionized my life and ministry. Echoes of these messages are found throughout this book.

For forty-three years of marriage, I have observed Morag's simple faith that the Bible is God's word, Jesus is God's Son, and the

Holy Spirit is our fruit producer. Morag has changed me more than I have changed her—hence this book!

Finally, I give utmost thanks for the saving life of Christ. Without Jesus I can do nothing, but in His strength I can do all things. Jesus is committed to me and all he asks is that I trust Him anywhere and everywhere, at any time and at all times, and in any place and every place!

Introduction

This is biblical Christianity! This isn't a different perspective: this is a biblical perspective. We are constantly having to separate cultural Christianity from biblical Christianity, and it is very difficult at times. When people have always done something one way, they assume that their way is correct, the only way.

Some churches I go to would not in a hundred years allow a guitarist to lead the worship. God does not have guitars in Heaven — didn't you know that? — so they would never allow it here on earth. Then there are people, like a lady in Scotland, who have said to me, "I want it the way it has always been." She assumed that organs had always been in churches. I pointed out to her that the organ came to Scotland's churches with Ira D. Sankey and D. L. Moody in the nineteenth century, and that many Scottish Presbyterians had spoken out against it, calling it "the devil's kist o' whistles" (that is, "the devil's chest of whistles"). That's what they called the organ then, just over a hundred years ago — and now, would you believe it, in Scotland, it's God's gift to the church!

I often wonder, if an alien visited this world and watched Christian television, what would the alien think Christianity was all about? Well, obviously high on the ratings would be that Christianity is fund-raising. That's what an alien might think Christianity basically is: fund-raising. Then the list could continue with a whole lot of other things: Christianity is a cheap way of shrinking hemorrhoids, curing backaches, and stretching short legs or shortening long legs. What would an alien think if it watched some of our church services?

Let me tell you a story that is not original with me. There was a man who had been unemployed for nearly two years. He wasn't a lazy layabout; he was very diligent in looking for work. He did not like being out of work, but try as he would, he could not find employment. He went once a week to the Employment Office to check for jobs, and the rest of the time he looked himself. He was getting discouraged, but one day he walked into the Employment Office and saw the clerk who always attended to him sitting at his desk with a line of people waiting. The man caught the clerk's eye and got the impression that the clerk had some good news for him. When he got to the front of the line, sure enough, the clerk said he had a job for the man.

"Fantastic! What is it?"

The clerk was a little hesitant, and said, "Well, it is different."

"That doesn't matter—I have been unemployed for two years! What is it?"

"I think that you would really be good at this."

"But what is it?"

"Well," said the clerk, "we have had a call from the zoo and their monkey has died and they are not going to get delivery of a new monkey for six months. The zoo is wondering if we could find some-one who would dress up in a monkey suit, go into the cage, and just act the monkey. I really think you are the man for the job."

"That is different," said the unemployed man, "but I will have a go at it. When do I report?"

"You start at 8:00 o'clock on Monday morning and you have to be in the cage by nine."

"I will be there."

So come Monday morning at eight o'clock, the man was at the zoo, where he was taken into the dressing room and given his monkey suit. He pulled the monkey suit on, put the head on, and looked in the mirror. He thought he looked different and that he had never seen himself look like this before, but decided, "Not to worry, I'll have a go and do my best." At nine o'clock on Monday morning, he was in the cage; by ten o'clock he was absolutely enjoying himself. Never by ten o'clock on a Monday morning had so many people crowded around just to look at him.

As the weeks passed, he thought that he had better learn some tricks. So, he learned to swing on the trapezes, and as more days went past, he put a somersault in between each trapeze. By the time he had got this down to a fine art, the crowds were coming by the hundreds to the zoo to see this phenomenal monkey. In fact, the zoo was really thinking of cancelling its order for the real monkey!

One day, when the man was really swinging on the trapezes, his hand slipped and, instead of catching the next trapeze, he went straight up in the air and over into the next cage. As he landed he realized that he was in a lion's cage. The lion, which had been in the corner, got on its feet. The man-monkey quickly looked around the cage and noted that there were no trapezes, no ladders, and no trees; the walls were very high, and there was no way to escape. The crowd that had been looking into the monkey cage called to the others that the monkey was now in the lion's cage. By this time the lion was moving slowly toward the man in the monkey suit, who was backing into the corner and thinking frantically about what to do. He was just at the point of shouting for help when the lion said, "Shut up or you'll get both of us fired!"

Now, does that ring a bell with you? Isn't that what many Christians do? You maybe did it this morning: got up and put on your Christian suit and mask and went to church or work or school, not wanting anyone to know what you are really like inside. Yet inside, you are no more a Christian than you are able to fly. Or you live with this day by day, this mask that you wear and the life that you don't have. You long to be alive on the inside and real on the outside.

If it is not real life on the inside, it is fake on the outside.

GENESIS MAN

Malcolm Muggeridge, in "Western Civilisation: To Be or Not to Be?," makes the following comment: "The real crisis is, thus, about man's relationship with his Creator rather than with his energy supplies, his currency, and gross national product, his sexual fantasies, and other passing preoccupations with which the media interminably concern themselves. These are essentially trivial matters" (speech delivered for the Pepperdine University Great Issues Series, Los Angeles, California, October 30, 1978).

No greater question can be asked than, "Is there a God?" The answer determines how a person lives. In the West today, God and His absolutes have been rejected, with the result that humankind has lost its way, and now the question that must be asked is: What went wrong? To answer that, we need to go back to the beginning, to Genesis.

Mankind Was Created in the Image of God

GENESIS 1:26–27

> [26] Then God said, Let us make man in our image, in our likeness, . . .
>
> [27] So God created man in His own image. In the image of God He created him, male and female He created them.

Who created man? God did. God created man—and He created man in whose image? His own image. And in whose likeness? His own likeness.

It Is an Image of Holiness Providing Freedom for Fellowship

We have to ask ourselves: What is that image? If you were to check through the Bible, you would find tremendous truths about God. God is a righteous God, God is a loving God, God is a faithful God, God is a giving God, God is an all-knowing God, God is an omnipotent God, God is a omniscient God and an omnipresent God. These are truths about God, about His essence or His attributes. The truth that governs all others, that permeates all others, is that God is *holy*. "Holy, Holy, Holy is the Lord God Almighty" (ISAIAH 6:3).

God is a holy God. He is holy in His mercy, holy in His grace; holy in His justice, holy in His love, holy in His omnipotence, holy in His omnipresence. God is a holy God. What stops men and women, boys and girls, from having a relationship with God today? Sin, because holiness and sinfulness cannot be in fellowship. They do not mix. Holiness and sinfulness do not walk hand in hand. God who is holy created Adam in His image, as holy, so that in the beginning Adam had freedom for fellowship with God.

It Is an Image of Personality Providing the Ability for Fellowship

There is another great truth about God: God is a personal God. God is not just an essence of the truths about Himself. God is a personal God.

What do we mean by *personal*? We mean that He possesses the basic characteristics of personality, intellect, emotion, and will. With His intellect He planned the universe. He has emotion: with emotion He loves and He hates. With His will, He says, "I make known the end from the beginning, from ancient times, what is still to come.

God is a personal God,

and God who is personal

created man in His image,

personal.

I say: My purpose will stand, and I will do all that I please" (ISAIAH 46:10). God is a personal God, and God who is personal created man in His image, personal. It is the personality of God and the personality of Adam that provided the ability for fellowship, the ability to relate one to the other.

I stay in many homes on my travels. It is interesting to watch the husband arrive home from work in the evening. Guess who meets him at the door? That's right, the dog. It's the dog that comes running to the door. It's the dog that barks; it's the dog that jumps up and licks his face; it's the dog that gets patted; it's the dog that gets its ears ruffled. Then the husband walks past his wife in the kitchen and grunts hello! The interesting fact is that when he is finished with the dog he says, "Sit," and that is it—finished. When he wants more attention, he says,

"Here boy, here boy." He does not discuss with the dog how the grass is going to be cut, he doesn't discuss with the dog where they are going on vacation, he doesn't discuss with the dog how they are going to pay their bills, he doesn't discuss with the dog where the children are going to school; that is what he does with his wife. You don't relate to a dog personality to personality as you relate to a human being personality to personality. Between humans, that relationship is mind to mind, emotion to emotion, and will to will. (I once told that story and a wife went home and told her husband all about the dog running to the door. He said, "Honey, when you come running to the door with your tail wagging like that dog I'll kiss you and ruffle your hair!")

God who is personal created Adam personal. He gave Adam a mind that we might know God. He gave Adam emotion that we might feel God. He gave Adam a will that we might obey God. In the beginning, Adam created in the image of God walked and talked with God and reflected the likeness of the God who had made him. What stops us from reflecting the likeness of God? It is the fact that we, prior to becoming Christians and even after becoming Christians, are like dirty and warped mirrors that show dirty and warped images. But God created Adam, in the beginning, holy and upright in his personality, so that as Adam lived he reflected accurately the likeness of the God who had made him.

**The Result: The Creature Man Was
a Living Visual Aid of God His Creator**

In GENESIS 2.15–17 we read, "The Lord God took the man and put him in the Garden of Eden to work it and take care of it. And

Right Relationship, Right Behavior

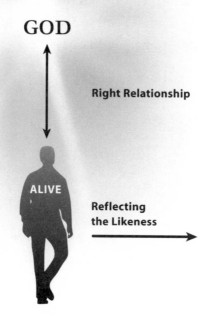

Then God said, "Let us make man in our image, in our likeness."
So God created man in his own image.

—GENESIS 1:26a, 27a

the Lord God commanded the man, 'You are free to eat from any tree in the garden: but you must not eat from the tree of the knowledge of good and evil, for when you eat of it you will surely die.'"

Now, what was Adam like before he ate from the tree in disobedience? He was alive in his relationship with God and alive in his behavior, accurately reflecting the likeness of God—as was Eve, the wife that God had given him. To discover what God means by life and death, we need to look at Adam and Eve as they lived before they disobeyed. Life is not swinging from the chandeliers; if you can do it, good for you, but some of you will never, ever be able to do it again! Those days have gone, but have you stopped living? No. You express your physical life in a different way now. Perhaps you get up early in the morning now and you go fishing, catching fish where before, when you were young, you chased girls! But you are still alive. So physical life changes.

Life, in the Bible, is a relationship with God; death is always separation from God.

There was a time when some of you had little children and you looked after them; now they are bigger and they are looking after you. Life changes—but God is not talking about physical life, even though you cannot divorce what He is talking about from the physical, because all that we do we express in the physical. What life is He talking about? Life, in the Bible, is a relationship with God; death is always separation from God. If you had seen Adam and Eve living in the Garden of Eden, prior to their disobedience, by watching their behavior and relationship one to the other, you would have been able to tell what their Creator God was like. They were created in His image to reflect His likeness. You would have seen them living in love, telling you that their Creator was a God of love. You would have seen them living in joy, telling you that their Creator was a God of joy. You would have seen them living in peace, telling you that their Creator was a God of peace, because He created them in His image to reflect His likeness!

What has He got against us today? We give wrong reflections; we give wrong information about the God who made us because of our sin. God said to Adam and Eve, "The day you disobey me you will die"; that is, you will be separated from me.

Mankind Disobeyed the Command of God

The Command That Was Given

GENESIS 2:15–17 reads: "The Lord God took the man and put him in the Garden of Eden to work it and take care of it. And the Lord God commanded the man, 'You are free to eat from any tree in the garden: but you must not eat from the tree of the knowledge of good and evil, for when you eat of it you will surely die.'" This was the direct command from the Creator God, the one who had created Adam in His image and His likeness. Obedience to this truth would have kept Adam in freedom; disobedience put him into bondage.

The Consequence of Disobedience

The Bible mentions three deaths: physical, spiritual, and eternal. Each one teaches separation. *Physical death* is the separation of the soul and spirit from the body. Those who have had a death in the family know that it is not a pleasant situation. I remember that when my mother died, I arrived home after midnight, and I went with my wife, Morag, into the room where my mother's body lay. The first thing I said was, "That is not my mother." I did not see the lady who had birthed me, fed me, kissed me, cuddled me, taught me, disciplined me, disciplined me, and disciplined me (did you have a mother like that, too?). That lady was gone. All that was left was the old tent she used to live in. Her soul/spirit was gone. But was she alive? Yes! The Bible teaches that the believer is absent from the body and present with the Lord. Physical death is separation of the soul/spirit from the body.

Spiritual death is the separation of the human from the Creator. In the New Testament, we read in ROMANS 6:23, "The wages of sin is death." This is not a wage that will be paid one day in the future. It was paid when Adam and Eve violated God's original command—but let's not rush too fast.

Eternal death is the separation of the human creature from God forever, eternally.

The Conflict with Satan

In GENESIS 3:1–7, we also read: "Now the serpent was more crafty than any of the wild animals the Lord God had made. He said to the woman, 'Did God really say?'" Satan is always the one who casts doubt on the words of God. He knew exactly what God had said, and he knew exactly when God said it, but he came along and asked, "Did God really say," artificially raising a question about what He really said. Satan misquotes God, asking, "Did God really say, 'You must not eat from any tree in the Garden?'" God never said that. God said that "You must not eat from the tree of the knowledge of good and evil, for the day you eat of it you will surely die." Satan comes along and asks, "Did God really say you must not eat from any tree in the Garden?"

Now, because Satan has got her confused and on the defensive, the woman comes up with wrong information. The woman replies to the serpent, "We must not eat from the trees in the middle of the Garden." That is *not* what God said. God did *not* say, "You must not eat from the trees in the middle of the Garden." He said, "You must not eat from the tree of the knowledge of good and evil." Eve is now on shaky ground, sinking sands, and tells the serpent, "God did say, you must not eat fruit from the tree which is in the middle of the garden and you must not touch it." No, He didn't say, "You must not touch it." She continues, "For the day you do you will die." The serpent replies, "You will not surely die?," directly questioning God's truth and challenging God's authority. "You will not surely die," the serpent says to the woman, "for God knows that when you eat of it your eyes will be opened, and you will be like God, knowing good and evil." Satan is always trying to say that God is wrong and he is right.

Have you ever noticed that when Satan tempts you, he never tempts you to do something third-rate? A temptation always seems first-rate, gold-plated, like you have got to do it. It is not until you have done it that it appears third-rate and tarnished. Have you ever noticed that? Even if you have been through the routine many times, every time Satan comes along to tempt you again, it's with something that is first-rate, gold-plated, that you have got to do. You know from experience that it is just not true, and yet you fall for it again. Satan's great concern and aim is this: Warp God's truth, tempt God's creature man and cause him to fall.

"When the woman saw that the fruit of the tree was good for food and pleasing to the eye, and also desirable for gaining wisdom, she took some and ate. She also gave some to her husband, who was with her, and he ate it. Then the eyes of them both were opened, and they realized they were naked; so they sewed fig leaves together and made coverings for themselves"—all because what had been normal, good, and correct now was warped and twisted and seen through totally different eyes. Adam and Eve had died.

Did they keel over with heart attacks? No, that is not what happened (though they were now in the process of dying physically). They died in the area in which they had been alive: spiritually. Where were they alive spiritually? In their relationship with God and their behavior like God. They died in their relationship with God and were separated from God.

What Is Life?

So what is life? Life is a relationship with the Creator God. What is physical life? It is the soul/spirit living in the body. If you are reading this book, you are alive, though some of you may have dozed off! There is spiritual life, which is a relationship with God. Eternal life is forever. When Adam died, he died in the areas in which he had been alive. He was alive in his relationship to God—he died; he was separated from God. He died in his ability to reflect the likeness of God because without God it is impossible to be godly. Now, instead of reflecting the likeness of the God who had made him—because he was separated, unplugged from God—he had to rely on his own resources, and he did not have the power necessary to reflect the likeness of God. He began to reflect his own likeness: dead, separated from God by his sin, immorality, impurity, greed, envy, jealousy, murder, and hate. That's what he began to do.

But it wasn't meant to be that way. Humankind was meant to have a relationship with God by faith in His Word. Do you know that the only way you can have a relationship with God is by faith? *That is the only way.* In any age, any stage, any dispensation, it is the only way. Before the Fall, after the Fall. Before the law, after the law.

Before the incarnation, after the incarnation. Before the Cross, after the Cross. Before the Spirit came, after the Spirit came. Faith is the only way to have a relationship with God. No one comes to God

Humankind was meant to have a relationship with God by faith in His Word.

except by faith. Faith is the only way, so Adam and Eve had to trust in the Word of God that had been revealed to them. As long as they lived in harmony with the Word of God and demonstrated faith by obedience in their lives, they were alive, and as they lived that lifestyle of obedience they reflected the likeness of the God who made them. They were alive and well.

Do you know what humankind is searching for today? Humans are searching for the life that Adam lost! They constantly try to fill the void that can only be filled by God. However, they try to fill it with everything else but God. You have tried it and I have tried it.

You can try to fill it with things. You know the sweatshirt that says, "He who dies with the most toys wins"? Rubbish! Do you know, and I say it carefully, that this generation in the West has never had so much and never been so discontented? It is so sad. We have never had so much but have never been so much in discontent. There are too many people, Christians included, who are trying to fill the vacuum that was created only for God. We search for life, we look for life because the only thing that will fulfill us is being alive in our relationship with God. When God is in our lives, we have the potential to become what we were intended to be. Adam died and he lost his relationship with God. He stopped living by faith, he distrusted the Word of God and he died, he was separated from God and could no longer reflect God's likeness. He could only reflect his own inadequacy. He was separated from God and thus he began malfunctioning.

Let me put it this way. Have you ever run out of gas while driving a car? Many of you who are men may remember that it happened to you when your wife was telling you that you were running low on gas. Most of you know that your wife is a better gas gauge than the one in the car. But you ran out. What do you do when you run out? Do you say, "Well, that is the end of that car, I had better look for another one"? No, you don't throw the car away. The problem is that you have a dead car! The tank is empty and the gas is separated from the car. The car was created to be indwelt and empowered by gas, and all it needs is more gas!

Oh, the interesting thing is this: You can push that car along a flat road. The more people you have pushing it, the more you can get it going pretty fast (you know, husband at the steering wheel, and the rest of the family pushing). It can be quite impressive, but you still have a dead car! When you get to a downhill, you can even fool people walking up the hill. You can all jump in. You can wave flags out the window, you can be singing songs as Dad steers the car. The people walking up the hill are wishing they had a car like that—they don't even know it is dead! You can fool them. Many people can be fooled in life. When they have a good job, plenty of money, good health, a good marriage, a good house, good kids, and a good car, and everything is going their way, it's like coasting downhill; many can do really well, but their spiritual tanks are empty! "Who needs God?" they say. Maybe they can fool the neighbors, for a while at least, but then they hit an uphill part in their lives. They lose the job, the money, the marriage; they get cancer; their kids start using drugs; they lose the big house and car and everything goes wrong. Then they find out that their tanks are empty and they don't have what it takes. They are dead—separated from God.

A businessman asked me if I would speak to his staff, and I readily accepted. One of his staff asked me if we could talk privately. She said, "Ian, when I was 22, I was in a serious car accident, my boyfriend was killed. I have gone through a lot of surgery and am now doing well. When that happened I lost my faith."

What do you say to someone like that? Well, I prayed and I said, as kindly as I could, "You know, when they built the Queen Mary, the Queen Elizabeth, and the QE2 they did not test them in dry dock. They didn't leave them in dry dock and get big hoses on them to see if they would leak. They got those ships out into the open ocean to put them through sea trials. These trials were not intended to sink the ship. These trials were to prove that the ship was seaworthy. The only way you can know whether your faith is real or not is when the pressures of life come, when you go through trials. Then you know if you are seaworthy or not. Can I ask you honestly, did you lose your faith or did you find you had none?"

She said, "Ian, I guess you are right, I had none."

Are you walking hand-in-hand with God, or are you out of contact with Him? Are you in a living relationship with God, or are you separated from Him? Are you wearing a monkey suit that looks real on the outside but has nothing on the inside? Christianity is all about a relationship with God, whereby we walk hand-in-hand with the God of this universe who is our loving, heavenly Father and know that we are His children.

Wrong Relationship, Wrong Behavior

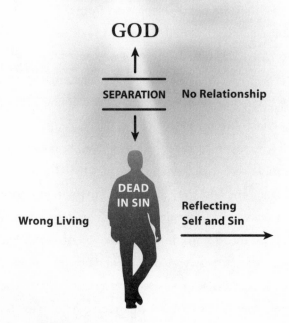

The wages of sin is death.

—ROMANS 6:23a

All have sinned and fall short of the glory of God.

—ROMANS 3:23a

TWENTY-FIRST-CENTURY MAN

2

We saw in the previous chapter that God created Adam in His image and in His likeness. God is a holy God and He created Adam holy. The holiness of God and the holiness of Adam provided the freedom for fellowship. Sin is what separates—but in the beginning God who is holy created Adam holy. God is also a personal God, with intellect, emotion, and will, and God created Adam personal, with intellect, emotion, and will. This creation of personality provided the ability or capacity for fellowship. Adam was given a mind that he might know God, emotion that he might feel God, and a will that he might obey God. So we discover that Adam walked and talked with God. He walked hand-in-hand with God. He had a living relationship with God. Before his disobedience, Adam was alive the way God intended him to be alive: created in His image to reflect His likeness! The creature, humankind, was meant to reflect the truths about the Creator God.

Adam disobeyed God and he died. Death in the Bible is always separation. Physical death is when the soul/spirit separates from the body. At spiritual death, the creature separates from the Creator. Eternal death is when the creature is separated from the Creator forever. Adam died in the areas in which he had been alive—not physically, though that death was enabled, but in other aspects of his being. He had been alive in his relationship with God, but he died and lost that relationship.

Man died, losing his relationship with God. Initially, he had reflected the likeness of the God who made him, but he died in his relationship to his Creator and thus suffered death in the way that he lived. He then did not have the power necessary to live correctly. Before that, he had lived by faith in the Word of God, trusting in God, who was his life and his light to reflect the likeness, but the light of God left him: the lights went out, and he became dead in sin, walking in darkness. Then he had only his own resources to depend on and he began to malfunction. Instead of love, joy, and peace, there was immorality, impurity, and greed. Man was dead.

Let me reiterate this so we fully understand the situation. Adam was separated from the life of God and was malfunctioning. Instead of reflecting the likeness of the God who made him, he reflected his own sin and his own inadequacy. Instead of reflecting holiness, he reflected sinfulness. This is what we read in GENESIS 5:1–3. It is a very simple statement but a very clear statement: "When God created man; He made him in the likeness of God. He created them male and female and blessed them. And when they were created, he called them 'man.'" Verse 3 says, "When Adam had lived 130 years, he had a son in his own likeness, in his own image, and he named him Seth." What was Adam's image? What was Adam's likeness? It was separation from God. Whereas once he had been absolutely upright in his personality, now he was warped and twisted. Whereas once he was holy, now he was sinful, no longer upright. Whereas once he had a relationship with God, now he was separated, out of contact with God.

Like kind bears like kind. You plant carrots, you get carrots; you plant tomatoes, you get tomatoes. It's the law of the universe, so sinful parents produce sinful children. It's really stupid for a mother to say to a child, "I don't know where you get this behavior!" (Mark you, it's usually the other side of the family that gets the blame. Isn't it amazing how, when we judge little kids, we attribute all the good traits to our side of the family and all the bad traits to the other side of the family?) Like kind bears like kind, so men and women who are out of contact with God produce children who are out of contact with God. Men and women who are warped and twisted in their will, intellect, and emotion will produce children who are warped and twisted in will, intellect, and emotion.

Now, I realize that when a little child is born, there is no way you would say that that little baby is a absolute monster, but the bias toward sin is resident in that child, and that is why no mother I know of has ever had to pick up little Jeannie at the age of six, place her on the countertop, and say, "Jeannie, you are so perfect I must show you how to tell a lie!" Or pick up little Johnny and say, "Johnny, you are so perfect I must show you how to throw a temper tantrum." Parents are always trying to get their children on course, because children naturally find it easier to go off course. Mothers and fathers, from early on, teach their children to tell the truth, not to steal, not to cheat, not to throw temper tantrums. Parents do not have to teach their children to lie or to steal or to otherwise misbehave! The inherent bias in our nature is to be off course. The need is to get back on course.

Even as Christians, we often find it easier to pass on bad news than good news. The whole point is this: Resident within us is the sin nature that begins to express itself very early in life, and it is biased to lead us off course.

Adam had children in his likeness, separated from God and malfunctioning. They were born physically alive but spiritually dead, separated from God. Thus, the main issue in life is man's relationship with his Creator. Man lost that relationship, and yet the need to worship is built into man, because he was created to worship his Creator. If man removes the Creator, he still must worship, so he attempts to fill that vacuum with something else—but it never satisfies. Like kind bears like kind, so we move from Genesis man to the day and age in which we live. We have to deal with twenty-first-century man: you and me.

God's Image Is Badly Marred in Mankind

What does the Bible say about us, humankind? What does it say concerning this situation? Let me turn to a verse that you may know very well, Romans 3:23: "There is no difference, for all have sinned and fall short of the glory of God." Well, there are differences, aren't there? There are tall people and small people. There are thin people and heavy people; there are young and old; there are different races; there are male and female. There are all different kinds of people. There is no way we are all the same! . . . or is there?

All Mankind Is Depraved

There is one area where each and every one of us stands equal and alike. "For there is no difference, all have sinned . . . " (Romans 3:23). You will notice that this is a completed act: "all *have* sinned." Like kind bears like kind, so the problem is that we are all sinners. We have this sin nature within us, passed on from generation to generation. "All have sinned": When Adam sinned, the human race sinned. When Adam fell, the human race fell. You can see the evidence of sin in every nation, on every continent, and in every culture. It is one of the easiest problems to diagnose. Of course, it is explained away on the basis of poverty, conditioning, environment, and social distinctions. Call it what you may, stealing is stealing, lying is lying, adultery is adultery, and murder is murder.

All of Mankind's Personality Is Depraved

Open a Bible and look at EPHESIANS 4. Not only does all humankind fall short of the glory of God, all of humankind's personality is depraved, marred, sinful: the mind, the emotion, and the will. EPHESIANS 4:17–19 says, "So I tell you this, and insist on it in the Lord, that you must no longer live as the Gentiles do, in the futility of their thinking. They are darkened in their understanding"; their intellect is darkened—and they are "separated from the life of God because of the ignorance that is in them due to the hardening of their hearts." Their hearts are hardened; they are debased. "Having lost all sensitivity, they have given themselves over to sensuality so as to indulge in every kind of impurity, with a continual lust for more." Their will is bent toward evil.

This is what the Bible says about our personality. When Adam sinned, he didn't lose his intellect. When Adam sinned, he didn't lose his emotion. When Adam sinned, he didn't lose his will. His intellect, emotion, and will did, however, become tainted with sin. Now, with a darkened mind, he can plan good and bad. With a debased emotion, he can love and lust. With a will bent toward evil, he can do whatever he wants within the circle of freedom—the free will—that God has given him. The end result? Humankind is in a mess.

When I was growing up, I remember my mother telling me that there was crude sin and cultured sin. I know now what she meant.

We can always look at the prostitutes, the pimps, the murderers and drug dealers, and the rest in the inner-city, red-light areas for "crude" sin: the obvious, undisguised sin. In suburbia, you will find the same things going on, but at a "cultured" level, and it doesn't seem so bad, because it's hidden or disguised. As far as God is concerned, though, sin is sin, whether crude or cultured, and it stinks in his nostrils. All have sinned and continue to fall short. Man with a darkened mind claiming to be wise has become a fool, the Bible says.

Some years back, I spent two weeks in high schools in Perthshire, Scotland, taking assemblies, religious education classes, and social education classes. I was teaching as clearly as I could the evidence of and necessity for a Creator in the creation: the overwhelming evidence in the design demanding a Designer; the obvious evidence in the order necessitating intelligence. I told these students that when I was at the University of Illinois, taking a week's evangelistic outreach with Inter-Varsity, about the second or third session on the third day, a student came up to me and said something like, "You see, I can't believe, Ian, because I am an intellectual."

"Oh," I said, "really, do you think I am a dummy?"

"Well, not really, but you see I am an intellectual."

What was this student saying? He was saying that he is intelligent, so he can't believe Christianity. He was saying that I am not intelligent, that I have kissed my brains goodbye! I said to him, "The more intelligent you are, the easier it should be to believe, because the more you discover, you don't get less evidence for God, you get more evidence for God."

When I was with a research scientist studying with brown bears in Minnesota, I went out to his laboratory, which was very interesting. We discussed many topics and he eventually said, "You see, the area which destroyed all my belief in God was genetics."

Now, I am no research scientist, but I can read like other people, so I said to him, "You are kidding! Everything I read about genetics indicates that more and more scientists are saying the incredible genetic code is so unbelievable that there is no way it could have happened by chance. Are you really going to tell me," I said, indicating the Apple computer that was sitting beside me, "that if we switched this computer on and an amazing program comes up on it, you would be willing to say that it just happened by chance? No, you know that someone programmed it."

The Result Is That Mankind Is Dead in Sin

Look at the program in the genetic code: what astounding evidence that somewhere there is an intelligent programmer! When you come to the point of saying all of that happened by chance, you demonstrate a darkened mind and debased emotion, and often a will bent toward evil. No wonder Paul wrote to the Ephesians, "As for you, you were dead in your transgressions and sins" (EPHESIANS 2:1). Mankind is dead, separated, in his relationship with God and dead, separated, in his ability to live and behave correctly.

Some of the things we read in the news and in research today are horrific. Some time back, a conference was held at Dundee

University, in Scotland, attended by personnel from the U.S. Federal Bureau of Investigation, U.S. police forces, and psychiatrists/psychologists, along with U.K. police, doctors, social workers, and psychiatrists. Their discussion centered on the incredible upsurge within Britain of the occult and the misuse, abuse, and abduction of children for cult worship and practices. The amazing thing is that if any preachers had mentioned this a few years ago, they would have been laughed out of court and out of the pulpit. Now it is not the preachers who are dealing with it, it's the police, the doctors, the psychiatrists, the professionals, the helpers, and the youth workers. Suddenly it is an issue.

Where does this debased behavior, this evil come from? Emotions that are debased. I saw a television report about a man from Florida who had killed 70 cats and kept a scrupulous, logical record of his deeds. When asked why he did this, he answered simply that he didn't like cats.

Where does this horrific behavior come from? Debased emotion and a will bent toward evil. Have you ever wondered why there are some people who seem to keep going off course, no matter how much others try to help them to get on course and stay there? They are never happier than when they have everyone else going off course along with them. All of us know that in whatever area of life we have a problem, if we feed it, it gets stronger; there is a continual lust for more.

The Bible gives a dark view, or maybe a more honest view, of the problem. Humankind is separated from God and humankind is depraved in every area of personality. Now, some of you may react with discomfort to this: "I thought I would read about love, joy, peace, patience, goodness, gentleness, and meekness." Those things are meaningful only if what the Bible says is true. There is only good news in relationship to bad news.

Mankind Is Malfunctioning in Living and Behaving

Malfunction in life and behavior is apparent in many areas.

It Is Seen in Lawlessness

In 1 JOHN 3:4 there is an interesting statement: "Everyone who sins breaks the law; In fact, sin is lawlessness."

I was in a school in Glasgow, Scotland. One of the senior pupils was giving me a hard time. His father was an atheist, his uncle was an atheist, and he was an apprentice atheist, so he was throwing all he could at me. Then he said something like, "Your God is just a big party-pooper. He thinks up Ten Commandments to spoil anyone having fun."

I happened to be looking out the window at that moment and saw a game of rugby taking place. I said to him, "See that game of rugby? Let me ask you an honest question. If we were to remove all the rules of the game and just let fifteen players from each side, thirty in all, playing on the field, give them an inflated piece of leather called a ball and say all right, have a game. You have no rules. Tell me, what would you have?"

He was honest enough to say that you would have chaos. I said, "If you were to remove the Ten Commandments from society, I want to tell you that you would get the same result: chaos in people's lives and anarchy in our society."

In every area of humanity and civilization that removes or ignores God's Ten Commandments, that is what eventually happens. There is a breakdown of law and order; instead of a life that is meaningful, you have life that is falling apart. God's commandments were never intended to spoil life, they were given to protect life.

It is the same for a person driving a car. The rules of the highway are not intended to spoil your journey. The red light is not meant to ruin your trip, though if you left late and every light on the way to your destination turns red, it is a bit annoying. That's not the red light's fault, that's your fault for leaving late.

Here's the point: The moment you break a rule of the highway, you endanger your life and the life of anyone else in your vicinity. Nothing in the rulebook can force you to obey the rules. In Scotland, the rule says drive on the left-hand side of the road, but that rule cannot *make* you do it; if you want, you can drive on the right-hand side of the road. All I say is watch out. The rulebook says to stop at the red light, but the rulebook has no power that will *make* you stop at the red light. In the end, though, the rules are good because they protect you during your journey from A to B, and if everyone follows the rules of the highway, you have the safest roads in the country. However, if everyone breaks them, what you have got? Chaos and danger.

God gave us Ten Commandments. Are they just ten arbitrary commands that He thought up? No. They are a projection of His own character of holiness. Do you know why He says "do not steal"?

Because He is not a thief, and he created you in His image to reflect His likeness. Do you know why He says "do not lie"? Because He is a God of truth, and He created us in His image to reflect His likeness, and He does not want us to lie. Do you know why He says "do not commit adultery"? Because He is a God of purity, and He created us in His image to reflect His likeness. That is why!

God's rules are there to protect us from the cradle to the grave. They are not there to spoil life. The Bible says that God's law is like a mirror. Did you look in the mirror this morning? Sure you did, with wonder, love, and praise. There you were going through

> *God's rules are there to protect us from the cradle to the grave.*

your morning mantra, "Mirror, mirror, on the wall, I am really not too bad at all!" Come on, you know that when you looked in that mirror, you saw exactly what you were like. That is why some of you shiver and vow that no one will see you like that. Did any of you get up and look in the mirror and say, "I have always wanted my hair like this"? I doubt it! Most of the time, we look in the mirror and say, "Oh my goodness me!" So what do you do? Well, you try and deal with the issue. The men shave (at least some of them do) and comb their hair the way they want it. The women put on their makeup and fix their hair and get themselves as much as possible the way they want to look. So the mirror reflects you accurately; it shows you what is wrong and needs to be corrected, but it never deals with the problems.

And that's the point. God's law is like a mirror. If you look into God's law, you will see exactly what you are like. When it says "do not lie," what do you see? When I was younger, I saw a liar. When it says "don't take my name in vain," what do you see in the mirror? I saw someone who tried very hard not to use God's name wrongly. When it says "don't steal," what do you see? I used to see a thief. "Don't commit adultery": what do you see? God's law will reflect you accurately.

Sometimes laws annoy us. You know that the speed limit is 30 miles per hour (mph) in a built-up area and 65 mph on the open highway. Isn't it amazing how it annoys you? You routinely drive 35–40 or 75–80 mph. Rules annoy us.

The classic instance is when you see a sign that says "Wet paint, don't touch." So you touch and say, "So it is!" God's laws actually irritate some of us, if not all of us, because we have a sinful nature that leads us off course. When He says not to do something, it is amazing how that affects us and how often we react to the contrary. God's commandments were never intended to spoil life; rather, they are to protect it. That is what they are there for. But they are also mirrors, which reflect us accurately as we are on the inside. What we discover is that we all fall short.

Are you the man you ought to be? Are you the woman you ought to be? I know you could probably say that you are not as bad as you could be, but can you say that you are as good as you should be? How many people could stand up and say, "Since the day I was born, I have lived a perfect life in every area of my being. My family agree with me 100 percent and say this is right: 'I have never, ever seen any evidence of wrong in his/her life.'"? Would anyone claim that?

Are you the man

you ought to be?

Are you the woman

you ought to be?

It Is Seen in Falling Short of God's Glory

As we noted earlier, the Bible says that "all have sinned," and then it says, "and fall short of the glory of God." That is a continuous tense. We have sinned (completed act), and we continue to fall short of the glory of God. Here is a key statement, an absolute "must" to understand, because if you fail to grasp this you miss the whole emphasis.

Glory is a word often used in old hymnology to mean heaven. "When I get to glory" means "when I get to heaven." In the Bible, however, *glory* almost always indicates reflected likeness. All have sinned and continue to fall short of the glory—that is, the reflected likeness—of God. Humankind was created in His image to reflect His likeness. All have sinned, so we fall short of reflecting His likeness. We were created in His image to reflect His likeness, but we fall short of the reflected likeness of God.

This is interesting wording, especially because it does not mean that every one of us is the same. The actual Greek word refers to a person firing an arrow that falls short of the target; it misses. You know there are many people who fall short more than others; there are many people who are better than others. If you were asked to think of someone you are better than, most of you could name someone right away! We all know people we are better than. Do you know why? It makes us feel good!

How about having a look around for people who are better than we are? That doesn't make us feel quite so good, even though we all fall short. It is not that we are as bad as we could be, it is that we are not as good as we should be!

Here's a ridiculous illustration. Suppose we all went down to the Atlantic Ocean to swim across to Scotland. Some of you will not even go in; for some of you, it's too cold (anything under eighty degrees means you will not go in). Some older people will not go in because they have a hole in the seat of the swimsuit and they are embarrassed. Others won't go in because they are certain they won't make it, and decide not even to try.

Eventually, some of us will jump in and start swimming. At first, we all do quite well, but one by one, people sink. For the sake of the illustration, suppose that I and a local pastor friend are left swimming. Eventually, I go under. My pastor friend will not give up; he keeps going, but half a mile from the Scottish shore, it is too much for him, and he goes under, too.

Who made it to the other side? No one. Even the one who went the farthest did not reach the goal, any more than the person who did not even go into the water. But in comparison to other people, my friend did much better than the rest, I did better than the people behind me, and they did better than the people who didn't even try. So in the end, it comes to this: Yes, many of us try to improve our lives; we don't want to be as bad as we could be, and for various reasons and in various situations we do improve. In the end, though, none of us by our own effort alone can match up to God's standard, reflecting His likeness of holiness. We don't have it. No matter how hard we try, we will still fall short, for all have sinned. All fall short of reflecting the likeness of God.

It Is Seen in Unbelief in God's Son

The Bible says not only that we break the law, but also that we sin in another area. In fact, the greatest sin the Bible ever mentions is not that of breaking God's law, which actually violates His character, but the sin of unbelief, rejecting His provision for our sin in the person of Jesus Christ. "For God so loved the world that He gave His one and only Son, that whoever believes in Him shall not perish but have eternal life" (JOHN 3:16); "The Lord is not slow in keeping his promise, as some understand slowness. He is patient with you, not wanting anyone to perish, but everyone to come to repentance" (2 PETER 3:9); "Everyone who calls on the name of the Lord will be saved" (ROMAN 10:13). God sees man in his sin, with a darkened mind, debased emotion, a will bent toward evil, and falling short of the likeness that we were created to reflect. He sees us in our sin and sends His Son to die for us, to pay the price, to satisfy God's justice to make a way to God.

> *The greatest sin of all is rejecting God's provision for our sin.*

This is the most important point for fallen humankind: *There is a way back to God.* We are reconciled to God through the death of His Son. God was in Christ restoring lost men and women to himself. Jesus came to make a way back to God for humanity. The greatest sin of all is rejecting God's provision for our sin.

The Bible reads like this: The one who believes in Him is not condemned. He who believes not is condemned already because he has not believed. He who believes in Him has everlasting life. He who does not believe shall not see life but wrath of God. The Bible clearly says, "God so loved the world that He gave His one and only Son, that whoever believes in Him shall not perish but have eternal life" (JOHN 3:16).

When people ask me why God doesn't do something about the mess the world is in, I give them the same answer every time: "He has, he has. He sent His Son to take our place, to pay our price, satisfy God's justice, and create a way back." Jesus answered, "I am the way and the truth and the life. No one comes to the Father except through me" (JOHN 14:6). "Salvation is found in no one else, for there is no other name under heaven given to men by which we must be saved" (ACTS 4:12). "Everyone who calls on the name of the Lord will be saved" (ROMANS 10:13).

Let me ask you: Have you ever come and repented of your sin and put your faith in the Lord Jesus Christ and invited Him into your life to be your Savior? Whoever shall call upon the name of the Lord shall be saved, set free, liberated, so that once more they can begin to reflect the likeness of the God who made them.

God created man in His image and in His likeness. I suggest that this image was twofold. It was of holiness, because God is holy. What keeps men and women from having a relationship with Him today? Sin. God created man in the beginning, so that there might be the freedom for fellowship. That deals with His essence. His holiness touches every area of His essence. But God isn't just essence, God is also a person, which means that He possesses the basic characteristics of personality. Therefore, God created man in His image holy and personal.

God gave man a mind that he might know Him, He gave him emotion that he might feel Him, He gave him a will that he might obey Him. In his original condition and situation, Adam walked and talked with God. But God said, "The day you disobey me, Adam, you will die." This simply means that mankind, Adam and Eve, was alive the way God intended us to be alive. It simply means that they were to live by faith, and we reiterate that you always, *always* know God by faith.

A teacher once asked her class, "What is faith?" A little guy stuck up his hand and said, "Faith is believing in things you know aren't true." The sad fact is that many non-Christians actually think that. One of the things I have to fight in schools is the concept that

> *Faith is trusting the evidence that is there and can be verified; trusting it and discovering the reality that comes from it.*

science is based on facts, but religious believers operate on faith, so we believe and trust in and hope for something for which there is no basis. That isn't faith. That is not faith in the slightest. Faith is trusting the evidence that is there and can be verified; trusting it and discovering the reality that comes from it. In a simple way, you are sitting in a chair by faith (some of you with more faith than others). You put your trust in the evidence: you know that a chair is made to hold you and now you have discovered the reality—it does hold you.

You and I check the evidence that is available. The Creation demands a Creator, the design demands a Designer; that is reasonable. The order within creation demands intelligence; that is reasonable. That intelligent, creative Designer has invaded this planet in the person of Jesus Christ. He fulfilled the prophesies, performed the miracles, and rose from the dead; we put our faith in that evidence and discover the reality that He is alive and He lives in our lives!

Faith is the way you and I have a relationship with God. It's not wishful thinking, as in Scotland when we say, "I have faith that it is going to be a sunny day on Saturday." That isn't faith, that is just wishful thinking. We have three months of winter and nine months of bad weather!

So, faith is a relationship according to the Word of God, a lifestyle of obedience that reflects the likeness of God. In the beginning, Adam and Eve lived in such a way that their relationship one with another portrayed the facts concerning the God who had made them. They lived in love, demonstrating that their Creator God is a God of love. They lived in peace, demonstrating that their Creator God is a God of peace. They lived in truth, demonstrating that their Creator God is a God of truth. They were created in His image to reflect His likeness. Despite God's warning that "the day you disobey me, you die," man disobeyed God, disobeyed the Word of God, and violated the commands of God, with the end result that he died. He died in his relationship to God and died in his ability to function and behave correctly. Before, by faith, lived out in obedience, man reflected the likeness of the God who had made him; because of sin, which separated God from man, there was no power within man, because the One who had been his life and his light left him. Man was left on his own and with his own resources to reflect his own sin, separated from God and malfunctioning. So now man is dead. The Bible always describes it as dead in sin.

That is why, if you think of Christianity purely as getting into heaven, you have missed the whole point. The issue isn't getting man out of hell and into heaven. (By the way, when he is in hell, that is the end; that is eternal death.) The issue is that man is out of contact with God. What do you think salvation is all about? Getting human beings back into contact with God. They are malfunctioning and reflecting their own sin. What do you think Christianity is all about? Getting them functioning correctly again, to reflect the likeness of God.

We know this as the fruit of the Spirit, as Christlikeness, as godliness. You can't have the fruit of the Spirit without the Holy Spirit. You can't have Christlikeness without Christ. You can't have godliness without God. You can try to imitate it, but that's how Christians have nervous breakdowns. If you try to imitate Jesus, and live like Jesus, you have had it. Jesus rose from the dead to do for you what you cannot do for or by yourself. He said, "Without me you can do nothing."

For years I was told that I had to live for Jesus. That's wrong: He rose from the dead to live for me! He is risen from the dead to

That is what Christianity is all about: restoring the relationship with God and restoring the likeness of God.

live in me, so that where I am weak I might become strong; where I am wrong I might become right; where I am bad I might become good; where I am off course, I might become on course, indwelt, and empowered by the risen Christ. His strength is made perfect in my weakness. So the Lord Jesus Christ is the one who wants to change our lives, which are separated from the life of God and malfunctioning by our inability to reflect the likeness of God. That is what Christianity is all about: restoring the relationship with God and restoring the likeness of God. Oh yes, heaven is in the package—of course it is, because if you have Christ you have eternal life. You have His life, which had no beginning and no ending. A restored relationship, life that continues forever—eternity!

The King James Version and the Authorized Version of the Bible translated JOHN 3:16 as "everlasting life." It was changed to "eternal life" in the New International Version because that is the correct translation. Everyone has everlasting life because everyone lives forever. You live with God forever or without God forever. But whoever believes in the Lord Jesus Christ possesses eternal life. We possess His life, which has no beginning and no ending, and he who has the Son has life. We became an heir with God and a joint-heir with Christ. The relationship we now possess is eternal life now, it is His life in us now. One day I shall see Him and be like Him.

Destiny was never the issue with God, it was the destinee. It wasn't changing my destiny that concerned Him, it was changing me. Once I am changed, then my destiny is changed. Some people hope to get their destiny changed, even though they never change and just hope to get to heaven by the skin of their teeth. They sing little hymns to encourage them along the way: it's not an easy road we're traveling together, but it will all be worth it and when the roll is called up yonder I'll be there; right now it is pure hell, but one day it will be heaven. Jesus rose from the dead to make it heaven now in the midst of hell! That doesn't mean that there will be no problems, no difficulties, no need for discipline, and no need for obedience. All these things are necessary—but He wants to come in and meet us at our point of need. That is what Christianity is all about.

If we are dead in sin, what are our chances of rectifying our own problem? Zero. None. There is no chance. God has to take the initiative. We discover that God so loved the world that He gave His one and only Son, so that whoever believes in Him shall not perish but have eternal life. He becomes the gas for our tanks that makes us go; He is the fuel that gives us new life!

THE GOD-MAN

3

We go on to God's solution to man's problem. You will notice that the first chapter was "Genesis Man" and the second chapter was "Twenty-First-Century Man." This third chapter is about the God-man. Man's problem is that he is separated from God and malfunctioning, because he is dead in sin and walking in darkness. Thus, we need to look at what God's answer is to man's problem.

The Person of Jesus Christ

In ROMANS 1:3–4 we read: "Regarding His Son, who as to His human nature was a descendant of David, and who through the Spirit of holiness was declared with power to be the Son of God by His resurrection from the dead Jesus Christ our Lord." Did you get that? God's Son, by virtue of His human nature, was a descendant of David: that is His humanity. Through the Spirit of holiness, He was declared with power to be the Son of God by His resurrection from the dead: that is his deity. In Jesus Christ we have the God-man.

He was descended from David *and* he was declared to be the Son of God. We obviously have a mystery in the God-man, because Jesus Christ was and is the second person in the Godhead, who existed within that Godhead before time began. How God became man and still maintained His deity—was totally God and yet totally man—defies human understanding. What we have to do is accept God's truth on the basis of His revelation and seek to grasp it, understand it as well as we can, and believe it. What we can say is this.

Jesus Was Man—Humanity

His humanity was planned before time began, before the foundation of the world. We know this because of 1 PETER 1:20, which says, "He was chosen before the creation of the world, but was revealed in these last times for your sake."

"He"—that is, the Lord Jesus Christ—was chosen before the creation of the world, but was revealed in "these last times," the years that had just passed, "for your sake," for the sake of the believers who had come to trust in Him.

When was the decision made that the second person of the Godhead should come into this world, take upon Himself human form, die on a cross, and rise from the dead for humankind's sin? He was chosen before the creation of the world. Sometime in eternity past the Godhead (Father, Son, and Holy Spirit) held a conference and decided that the second person would be the one to take upon Himself human form and die for the sins of the world. He was revealed in these last times for your sake: Jesus' sacrifice wasn't a sudden afterthought. Rather, in eternity past, God foresaw the mess that humanity would get itself into and decided beforehand, within the unity of the Godhead, what to do about it.

Even more significant is REVELATION 13:8, which says: "The Lamb that was slain from the creation of the world." I know I am

jumping into that verse midstream, but this is mysterious and important. How in the world can you say that the Lord Jesus Christ, as we
know Him, the second person of the Godhead, was slain before the
creation of the world? It is tied in with what we said concerning God's
personality. He has a mind with which He thinks, He has emotion
with which He feels, He has a will with which He says, "I will accomplish everything I have decreed." What did He decree? Within the
Godhead, the decision was made that God, the second person, would
become man. It was decided that He would die for the sins of the
world, and so He is the Lamb that was slain for the sins of the world
before the creation of the world.

This also signifies that when God says something is going to
happen, it is as good as done, so He can talk about it as if it had already
happened. We can't keep our word like that, but God can. When God
says it is going to happen that God the Son will die on the cross for
the sins of the world, He is (already) the Lamb that was slain before
the creation of the world. He was revealed in these last times, and they
came to a place called Calvary and they crucified Him.

So, His humanity was planned before time began. It wasn't
some sort of afterthought when God saw the mess that humanity
had made. Not only was this humanity planned, it was prophesied.
This is fact. No Jew should ever have been taken by surprise when
Jesus arrived!

I am convinced that the church will be the same when He
comes the second time. Yes, the church will be the same at the Second
Coming. We can dissect why we believe premillennial theories or
amillennial theories or postmillennial theories, but in the end, the
issue isn't dissecting theology, it is being ready for His coming today.

For in such an hour as you think not, the Son of Man comes. The church should be aware that He is coming and in a real sense be ready and watching for His coming. Now, in North America people may not be as aware of this as we tend to be in Britain and parts of Europe. You know, we have voted several times for a European parliament, which is not a decision-making parliament, but don't kid yourself, they are making some pretty powerful decisions. No tariff barriers across the whole of Europe, with the potential of a greater monetary system than that of the United States. America is beginning to wake up. Things are beginning to happen, and the more I see them happening within the European arena, the more I see that His coming is near—but when did you last hear a message on the Second Coming?

His Humanity Was Prophesied in the Old Testament

The Old Testament contains more than 300 prophetic utterances concerning the coming Messiah, which, when broken down, cover 60 major subjects from His birth to His death. The Jews should have known for sure that the Messiah was coming, and coming soon, but He came to His own and His own received Him not. Incredible! So all these prophecies were given. The very first one is found in GENESIS 3:15. The theologians call it the *protevangelium*, that is, the first announcement of the gospel. This first announcement of the gospel describes the future seed of the woman battling with the seed of the serpent. The seed of the woman is going to suffer and the seed of the serpent is going to be defeated. In symbolic and pictorial language, this verse declares God's answer to man's need.

Seven hundred years before the birth of Jesus, MICAH 5:2 declared, "But you, Bethlehem Ephrathah, though you are small among the clans of Judah, out of you will come for me one who will be ruler over Israel whose origins are from old, from ancient times." In fulfillment of this prophecy, Jesus was born in Bethlehem!

Five hundred years before Jesus was born, ZECHARIAH 9:9 instructs, "Rejoice greatly, O daughter of Zion! Shout, daughter of Jerusalem! See, your king comes to you, gentle and riding on a donkey, on a colt, the foal of a donkey." Matthew, Luke, and John recorded the fulfillment of this prophecy as Jesus rode into Jerusalem on Palm Sunday.

Twelve hundred years before Jesus, David predicted that the Messiah would die a death by crucifixion (PSALM 22)—and when they came to a place called Calvary they crucified Jesus! All these prophesies were saying, "He is coming, He is coming; Emmanuel, the God with us." His humanity was planned before the foundation of the world and His humanity was prophesied throughout the Old Testament.

He Had a Human Body

Then Jesus came. He had a human body. In one sense, there was nothing freakish about it. Oh yes, there was a virgin birth. He wasn't flown in by six angels. He wasn't dropped by a stork. He had a normal birth: the simple statement in GALATIANS 4:4 says, "God sent his Son, born of a woman." He had normal growth. In fact, LUKE 2:52 says, "Jesus grew in wisdom and stature, and in favor with God and men." That is, He grew mentally, physically, spiritually, and socially. He had normal growth and development.

Christianity should touch the whole man, physical, mental, emotional, spiritual. I am not talking about doing aerobics to get firm for Jesus! Rather, this is about presenting our bodies as a living sacrifice, which is our spiritual worship. In the end, the only way you can express Christianity is with your body. Did you realize that? In fact, the only way you can express anything is with your body. You can think things, but that is not an expression. Eventually, anything

> *In the end, the only way you can express Christianity is with your body.*

you ever do, you have to do with your body. Some of you, if you had the chance, would leave your bodies at home and go to work on your own and give them a break. (Some of you leave your minds at home for a break!) You sleep with your body, you eat with your body, you work with your body, and you compete with your body, and on and on. You have to do everything with your body. That is why God says to present your body as a living sacrifice.

He Experienced the Limitations of a Human Body

Jesus was man and experienced all the limitations of His human body. The Bible say that He was hungry when tempted in the wilderness. He was thirsty at Sychar's well. He slept on the boat. He wept at the tomb of his friend Lazarus. He died on the cross.

Many a time we say, "Well, that was all right for Jesus, He was God." Hold it a minute. When He came into this world, He did not come to live as God. He came into this world to live as a man. At no time was He ever less than God, but He lived day after day as though He was never more than a man. He said, "By myself I can do nothing; I judge only as I hear, and my judgment is just, for I seek not to please myself but him who sent me" (JOHN 5:30). He came to live as a man— and how was man meant to live? By faith in the word of God, lived out in obedience to the will of God. Remember what God said to Adam: As long as you obey me you will live, but the moment you disobey me you will die. So mankind was created to live in dependence on God. The greatest sin in the world is the sin of living independent of God. That is humanity's basic, original problem.

That is why Jesus lived as the second Adam. The first Adam was a living being; the second Adam became a life-giving spirit. The first Adam was to live obediently by faith, but he disobeyed. The second Adam came to live obediently by faith and he obeyed. So anytime you encounter Jesus, you see what man is meant to be like. It wasn't easy for him. When he was hungry, he was hungry. When he was tired, he was tired. When he slept, man, did he sleep! You can imagine old Thomas running around that boat, saying, "I doubt if we are going to make it, boys, I doubt if we are going to make it, we are going to drown." (He really had a gift for doubting.) So Jesus experienced all the limitations of a human body, and he was tempted at all points, just as we are, yet began and remained without sin.

You see, the Lord Jesus Christ was truly human. He laid aside that which was rightfully His, His deity. He did not stop being God, but He laid aside the usage of His deity and He came to live as man. Nevertheless, He was still God, who through the Spirit of holiness was declared with power to be the Son of God by His resurrection from the dead. The greatest proof that Jesus is who He said He was, the Son of God, is His resurrection from the dead.

Jesus Was God—Deity

When my wife, Morag, and I returned to Scotland, after I graduated from Moody Bible Institute in 1969, I started working in schools. One of the things I quickly realized is that there is no use telling people to believe in someone whom they don't even believe exists. The one who comes to God must believe that He exists and that He rewards those who diligently seek Him. Too many times we find ourselves telling people to believe in someone they are really not sure actually existed. In Britain I heard all the allegedly scientific and philosophical arguments against Jesus having existed, against the Bible being God's Word, against there even being a God. So I started to read, and read all about the resurrection till it eventually dawned on me that, without my having planned to do this, I had so got to grips with the resurrection that I *could not disbelieve* that Jesus was the Son of God, even if I tried! I had become so grounded in the foundation of my Christian faith that I could not disbelieve, because the evidence for the resurrection is so overwhelming. That is why, if someone asks me if I have some doubts, I can say, "Absolutely none." That sounds awfully holy and priggish, doesn't it? Not if you get to grips with the foundation; you will know you are not going to sink.

Does that mean to say that every day I am on a spiritual high? Of course not (just ask my wife). I am not always on a spiritual high, but I tell you something: even when I have problems or pressures, I never, ever doubt my Christianity. Why? Because nothing can remove the evidence for the resurrection. That is the stability through the storm; the foundation on which I stand, which becomes my security against the pressures of life. One of the most important things to understand and believe is the resurrection of Jesus Christ—the God-man.

One of the most important things to understand and believe is the resurrection of Jesus Christ — the God-man.

The Facts of the Resurrection

Yes, He was man, but He was God and He rose from the dead. The key chapter on the resurrection is 1 CORINTHIANS 15. Read this chapter every day for a year; read it, take it in as a spiritual antibiotic! I tell you, it will begin to transform your thinking. It will renew your mind, and strengthen your mind on the great truth that Jesus rose from the dead.

How do we know He rose from the dead? The first reason or piece of evidence is that the tomb was empty. If you check out all the evidence from the Scriptures, you will discover that everyone admitted that the tomb was empty. There is not one person who said, "The tomb is not empty, the body is still in it." They all agreed that it was empty. That is why they had to find an explanation for its emptiness! The explanation of the Roman guards was that the disciples stole the body while the guards were sleeping. Well, you don't have to be a lawyer to know that that wouldn't stand up in court. If you were asleep, how can you say the disciples stole the body? What do you know about what is going on while you are asleep? (Be honest: sometimes you don't know what's going on when you are awake!) This reasoning just doesn't stand up—but isn't it amazing what people will say? They will even stray into stupidity and absurdity to try to disprove something. Meanwhile, the fact is that the tomb was empty.

The second reason we know that Jesus rose from the dead is that He made personal appearances. He appeared approximately 10 or 11 times over a period of 40 days, to crowds of more than 500 at one time. That is astonishing and incontrovertible. You cannot beat the real thing. Remember, ten of the disciples ran away; one of them, Peter, cursed and swore that he didn't know Jesus, and another one, Judas, hung himself. It's pretty clear that Jesus didn't have an enthusiastic bunch of disciples. When they saw Jesus, you would have thought they would have said, "Great, fantastic, wonderful!" What do we discover, though? When their women came back and said, "We have seen him," the disciples didn't believe them, but had to go check for themselves. Then, when Thomas hears, he doesn't believe it; he has to see the marks on Jesus' hands and the wound in His side. You discover that these frightened disciples had great reservations. They didn't believe that Jesus was going to rise from the dead, and it took a good bit of convincing to prove to them that He did. Finally, Thomas, when he is confronted by Jesus telling him to check out my hands and my side, gets on his knees and says "my Lord and my God." What convinces Thomas is the real thing.

The important thing is not Thomas saying "my Lord and my God," but Jesus saying, "Thomas, I am glad you believe. You believe because you have seen; happy are the people who will never see yet believe." The evidence is there for anyone who wants to investigate, and that is why you and I need to be intimately familiar with the evidence: so that we can defend our faith and so that we can build on our faith.

He made these appearances and caused an amazing change in the disciples. From men who ran away because of fear, they became men who were convinced through these appearances, and were willing to suffer whippings, beatings, stonings, lashings, shipwrecks, starvation, imprisonment, and martyrdom for their claim that they saw him alive! As Chuck Colson explained so well, when Watergate took place, some of the strongest men in the political world couldn't keep it quiet. They couldn't cover it up. They couldn't keep it a secret. They couldn't silence it. Before long, the secret was out, and even though each wheeled and dealed against the other to get time off, time out, they couldn't keep it quiet. These disciples, from tradition, all died for saying that they saw Jesus alive. Incredible evidence, to go the rest of your life in suffering. They didn't live the rest of their lives and make big bucks on it and have condos on the Sea of Galilee and conference tours on the Mediterranean and trips to the Holy Land—no, they suffered. That is more great evidence that Jesus was who He said He was.

Not only did Jesus' resurrection change the disciples, it also changed the day of worship. Do you ever wonder why we worship on a Sunday when the Bible says to remember the Sabbath day to keep it holy? A lot of people don't realize this. In Scotland, you will still see churches advertising Sabbath services, but they are held on Sunday; or Sabbath school, meaning Sunday school, but they are held on Sunday. They are not held on the Sabbath at all. Sabbath is the Saturday. So how did we start worshipping on the first day of the week when the law said remember the Sabbath day to keep it holy? We worship on the first day of the week, Sunday, because Jesus rose from the dead on a Sunday! We come to celebrate His resurrection. I have been in some churches where it wasn't a celebration, it was the rerun of a funeral. The early church came to worship on Sunday because He rose from the dead on Sunday and is alive. That is how Jesus' resurrection changed the day of worship.

Then there is the Christian's personal experience. Many people reading this book ten years ago would have been amazed if some-one had told them that they would become Christians. Many of you would have been amazed five years ago. Many of you would have been amazed if someone had told you last week! How do you explain your Christian experience? How do you explain this change within you? How do you explain when God answers your prayer? I have one of the funniest answers. I keep a prayer book. In fact, I have two prayer books. I keep a prayer book where I list things I am praying for; then I check them off when I get the answers. I put down the date and the check-off.

I remember the first time we got a car—telling no one, just praying for it. The Heralds Trust that I work for, they were praying and we were praying. I was out in my garden. My next-door neighbor said, "I am going to have to buy a new car."

I said, "Yes, I am praying about one as well."

He said, "What?"

I said, "I am praying for a new car."

He just looked at me and said, "Good luck to you!"

Morag and I went off to ministry abroad, and when we came back a new car was sitting in our driveway, given to The Heralds Trust by a close friend. Actually, the night I left the phone rang. The person on the phone said, "If my wife could see me right now she would kill me. I am standing in the house with my boots on and they are covered in mud as I have been in the garden, but God has been telling me for two weeks to buy a car for The Heralds Trust. If I don't do it now I will never do it." (Has God ever told you to do something and you put it off and put it off until eventually you never did do it?)

Here I am on the phone. He wants to buy The Heralds a car. I told him we had been praying for a car, we would be delighted to accept! So I went off to the United States and when I got back there was the car sitting outside the house. That night, I got into the garden to try to catch up with the weeding when out comes my neighbor, carrying a Bible. He came out and said to me, "What do I do now, Ian?"

When you look at these answers, how can you explain them if God doesn't exist? How do you explain these experiences if God isn't there? You can't. How do you explain the change in your behavior, the change in your home, the change in your family, and the change in your lifestyle if Jesus isn't the Son of God? You can't. One of the great truths of the resurrection is that He rose from the dead to come and live within me; I put my faith in Him and discovered that He is who He said He was and that He is changing my life from the inside out!

The Significance of the Resurrection

What is the significance of the resurrection? It is proof of the deity of Jesus. He is declared with power to be the Son of God by His resurrection from the dead.

What else? It is proof of our resurrection one day: because He rose, we will rise. Because He was raised from the dead, we will be raised from the dead. Jesus said, "I am the resurrection and the life. He who believes in me will live, even though he dies; and whoever lives and believes in me will never die" (JOHN 11:25–26). One day we will rise. He is going to raise us from the dead and He is the first-fruits of the resurrection.

This is what I find in ROMANS 8:11: "If the Spirit of him who raised Jesus from the dead is living in you, he who raised Christ from the dead will also give life to your mortal bodies through his Spirit, who lives in you." So, living within us is the person and the power of the resurrection. The Spirit who raised Jesus from the dead is the Spirit who lives within us, so the person and the power of the resurrection live within us. No wonder Paul could say, "I can do everything through him who gives me strength" (PHILIPPIANS 4:13).

In the beginning God created humankind in His image to reflect His likeness. It was an image of holiness, for God is a holy God, and an image of personality, for God is a personal God. Holiness provided the freedom for fellowship with God and personality provided the ability or capacity for fellowship with God.

God said, "The day you disobey me you die"; Adam disobeyed God and died. As we said, he didn't keel over with a heart attack. What did he do? He died in the specific areas in which he had been alive. He had been alive in His relationship with God and he died in his relationship with God—there was separation between God and man, between the Creator and the creature. He had been alive in his behavior, behaving the way God had created him to behave, which was to be a reflection of God who had created Him. Mankind was created to be a visual aid of God, but after disobeying God he became a visual aid of himself and his sin.

This carries over into normal family life as well. Isn't it amazing? We saw Olivia Skye, our granddaughter, three days after she was born. The first thing I heard my wife say was, "Isn't she like Steve!" How can a three-day-old baby look like a thirty-two-year-old man? We soon pick out family likenesses, and we align all the good ones with our side of the family and the bad ones with the other side of the family. That's why some of us are just a chip off the old block, so to speak. God created his children in the beginning to look like Himself. He created man to reflect His likeness. Sin came in, separating the relationship, so man died in his relationship. God, who had been his life and his light, left man. Remember what was said about Jesus when He came into the world: "In Him was life and that life was the light of men" (JOHN 1:4). There was a time when God lived within man and was his light and his life, but God left man and man died and the lights went out. After separation, he had no power to live the way he was created to live. He had only his own ingenuity, his own striving, his own endeavoring—but he falls short.

Man's problem is that he is dead in sin, separated from the life of God and malfunctioning in his behavior. Therefore, he himself cannot do anything to improve his own state of deadness. The need is for God to do something, and we know that God is the one who takes the initiative. For God so loved the world that He gave His

Son. God demonstrated his love for us in that, while we were yet sinners, Christ died for us.

I throw this next bit in for the benefit of wives, as a by-the-way. When a husband loves his wife, it is not just an emotion, it is action. So you love your wife: no doubt that is why you bring her home bouquets of flowers and boxes of chocolates as evidence that you love her, because love is action. How many of you have had bouquets of flowers and boxes of chocolates? Love is action!

God didn't just have warm feelings about us. God acted and God demonstrated His love for us in the most extreme way: while we were yet sinners, Christ died for us. Love is action. God did something about humanity's problem. He sent His Son, who was God yet was man, who was man yet was God. Although He was never, ever less than God, He came into the world to live as though He were never, ever more than a man. He made himself nothing, took upon Himself the form of a servant: He was made in the likeness of man. He became obedient unto death, even death on a cross.

Jesus is the one who is the answer to our problem.

Jesus is the one who is the answer to our problem. We need to look at the mission of Jesus Christ. I hope I have said enough for you to realize that Christianity is not getting you out of hell and into heaven. It is not just changing destiny, though we often reduce it to that. We ask people, "If you were to die tonight, where would you go?" We ask that even though we realize that 99.9 percent of the people we ask aren't going to die tonight. Then, if we do get them saved by this concept, we have to get them convinced that they are going to heaven—well, hoping they are—but having a desperately difficult time getting there.

God's concern is different. He deals with the areas of death, which are the real problem.

What are these problem areas? Humanity is out of contact with God. What do humans need? They need to be reconciled, restored to contact with God. Humankind is malfunctioning. What do humans need? They need to be regenerated to function correctly. That is humankind's need: that men and women, boys and girls, be restored back to a right relationship with God and regenerated to a correct behavior so that they are conformed to God's image and reflect God's likeness.

We have a desperate situation, particularly in the West, where many people say they are born again but there is no evidence of new life or new behavior. I know people who have evidence of new life but cannot tell you the moment they were born again. Some people will say, "Oh, then they are not saved." Nonsense! When most babies are born, their mothers know all about it. There are all different kinds of physical birth, from extremely easy to extremely difficult. I personally don't remember the day I was born. Do you? Do you think I care? I have a birth certificate that tells me I was born, but do I get all uptight because I don't remember the moment I was born? No, I know I am alive, therefore I was born. I know people who will tell you that in 2001 they did not believe and in 2007 they do believe. Somewhere in that period of time they crossed over from unbelief to belief. God knows when they were born into His family. He knows that moment. I tell you something, I don't have to worry or be concerned because people don't know exactly what moment they were reborn. I can see their lives being conformed to His likeness. I have got more worries with people who say they were born again on such and such a date, but there isn't one scrap of evidence of new life to authenticate their stories. There is something wrong.

The Mission of Jesus Christ

God's mission program is to restore humans to a right relationship with Himself, and to restore humans to correct behavior so that they reflect His likeness. That is what salvation is all about. It

God's mission program is to restore humans to a right relationship with Himself....

deals with the matters of death and restoration of life—and of course one day we shall see Him and be like Him, because He is our Father and we are His children who reflect the family likeness!

ROMANS 5:10 is one verse you should memorize. It succinctly states what Christianity is all about: "When we were God's enemies, we were reconciled to him through the death of his Son, how much more, having been reconciled, shall we be saved through his life!" Many years ago, I discussed this verse with our son, Steve, while I was still reading books to him. We were well past children's storybooks and on to simple apologetics, the defense of the Christian faith. We were also reading *His Image, My Image* by Josh McDowell (1993, Thomas Nelson, Inc.), which deals with having a good image of yourself in the light of biblical teaching. The point is not to think of yourself more highly than you ought, but to think of yourself as God has made you and thank Him for being you. In fact, Steve was about fifteen when he said to me one evening, "You know, Dad, I can actually read!"

I laughed and said, "Steve, I have loved reading to you and wondered how much longer I could keep going." At that time I was reading an apologetics book, and we came across one particular chapter which said that Christianity was a historic faith. I was trying to share with Steve that this didn't mean that Christianity was 2,000 years old; it simply meant that our faith has basis. It is based on historical, verifiable events, specifically the death and resurrection of Jesus.

"When we were God's enemies, we were reconciled to him through the death of his Son" (ROMANS 5:10). Jesus died on a cross for us. "How much more"—this should be underlined, there is something more important coming. Some of you will say, "Is there something more important than Jesus dying on the cross?" You might say, "No way." But how much more, having been reconciled, shall we be saved by his life. Jesus rose from the dead. He makes us alive by His life. He is no longer dead; He is alive, and He makes us alive by His life. So He died on the cross and He rose to life from the tomb. That is the historic basis of salvation. It is very important because, in the end, we do not believe a philosophy or a theology that has no basis; rather, we believe the historic fact that Jesus Christ died on the cross, from which the truth comes that He died for our sins.

We believe that He rose from the dead, from which the truth comes that He rose from the dead to give us spiritual life. What does this verse say? "When we were God's enemies." When did we become God's enemies? When Adam disobeyed God and died, when humanity was separated from God. When Adam disobeyed God and died, humanity began to malfunction. Like kind produces like kind: carrots produce carrots, dogs produce puppies, cats produce kittens, and so on. So also sinful men and women produce sinful boys and girls. We are born in sin and shaped in iniquity. We are enemies of God, separated from God. "When we were God's enemies we were reconciled to him through the death of his Son" (ROMANS 5:10). Jesus died on the cross to reconcile humankind, to make a way back to God so that lost men and women, boys and girls, might be restored to humanity's original right relationship with God! So that the Creator God and the creature humankind might once more walk hand-in-hand!

Jesus Came to Seek and to Save the Lost

What else do we discover? Jesus said, in LUKE 19:10: "For the Son of Man came to seek and to save what was lost." Jesus gave three parables to teach this truth: the lost coin, the lost sheep, and the lost son. He gave these three parables to indicate that He, the Son, came to seek and to save the lost, that is, men, women, boys, and girls who are out of contact with their Creator, God, because of sin.

Jesus is the one seeking and saving the lost; hence the story of the shepherd and the lost sheep. How many sheep were in the sheepfold? Ninety-nine. One was lost and that was the shepherd's concern, the one that was lost. He also had concern for the ninety-nine; he was glad they were safe in the sheepfold. Some of us, if we had been the shepherd, would have said, "What's one more? By the time lambing comes around next year we'll have another hundred anyway, and if they all have twins they will be back up to two hundred." That might be our attitude. Not Jesus. He went out looking for the one lost sheep. He wasn't willing for even a single sheep to be lost. God is not willing that any should perish, but desires that all should come to a knowledge of the truth.

If you come to Edinburgh, Scotland, and visit Holyrood Palace, you will look out on an extinct volcano called Arthur's Seat. D. L. Moody went there at the end of the nineteenth century. He preached a sermon on the Good Shepherd and the lost sheep. There were about 30,000 people listening to him, with no microphones, no loudspeakers, no enhancement at all. Of course, there were no cars or airplanes making noise, either. It was peaceful as he preached. Afterward, he turned to Ira Sankey and said, "Mr. Sankey, would you sing a song appropriate to the message?"

Sankey had torn a poem out of a British newspaper and put it in his pocket. He had been thinking about it all the way through the sermon because the poem was "There Were Ninety and Nine That Safely Lay in the Shelter of the Fold but One was Lost on the Hills Away Far Off from the Gates of Gold." (It was written by a Scottish lady named

Elizabeth Clephane, who lived from 1830–1869 and who also wrote my favorite hymn, "Beneath the Cross of Jesus"!) Although this poem had not been set to music, Sankey felt that this was the song he should sing. Sitting down at his little pump organ, Sankey started playing and singing, "There Were Ninety and Nine That Safely Lay in the Shelter of the Fold," making up the tune as he was actually singing it. Then he went on to the second verse, singing exactly the same tune as he had sung for the first verse; then the third verse and the fourth and the fifth. It had a tremendous impact, underscoring the wonderful truth that Jesus Christ is the Good Shepherd who is looking for the lost sheep, and He is not willing that any of them should perish. He came to seek and save the lost, those who because of sin are separated and out of contact with God.

I spoke to a girl not so long ago and asked her when she became Christian. She said, "I found Jesus four months ago."

I said, "Really? Where was He?" We sometimes give the impression that we found Him, as though He had been lost. No, He found us, *we* were lost. We need to keep that in mind.

Then there was the lost coin. A lady lost a coin, and could not find it in the clutter of her house. So, she began to sweep the house. (Mark you, if she had cleaned the house beforehand, she might not have lost the coin!) She swept the house until she found the coin.

Then there was a father whose son spent his inheritance early, so he left his family in shame. Still, the father was always looking, always longing for his son to come home. One day he saw his son far off and ran to meet him.

These three parables, which Jesus related, are all meant to teach God's concern for humankind. God is the initiator in salvation. Then there's this one other little truth. When the sheep was found, and the coin was found, and the son was found, what did they do each time? They rejoiced, they had a party!

The Bible says there is rejoicing in heaven over one sinner who repents. If churches would only have parties and food when people got saved, certainly in America you would be getting more people saved, because you sure do like food and parties. You might

He is out looking for the lost who are ... separated from Him, so that they might be restored ....

hear someone say, "We haven't had a party in this church for a while. What's the problem? No one saved? We had better get out there and get someone saved, I'm getting hungry." I think it would be a good idea. When people get saved, once a month, have a salvation dinner. Welcome them into the family. Have a party, welcome them in, clap them on the back and say welcome home. It would be great. The lost sheep was found and everyone rejoiced. The lost coin was found and they rejoiced. The lost son was found and they rejoiced. That is God's concern. He is out looking for the lost who are out of contact, separated from Him, so that they might be restored to contact with Him.

We are reconciled to God through the death of His Son. Jesus' death on the cross created the only way back to God. *There is no other way.* There is no other name under heaven given amongst men whereby we must be saved. Jesus said, "I am the way and the truth and the life. No one comes to the Father except through me" (JOHN 14:6).

The problem in our world is sin, which separates humankind from God. The good news is that "God was reconciling [reconnecting] the world to himself in Christ, not counting men's sins against them" (2 CORINTHIANS 5:19). "You see, at just the right time, when we were still powerless, Christ died for the ungodly" (ROMANS 5:6). "We see Jesus, who was made a little lower than the angels, now crowned with glory and honor because he suffered death, so that by the grace of God he might taste death for everyone" (HEBREWS 2:9).

The cross was essential for God's justice to be satisfied. "He did it to demonstrate his justice at the present time, so as to be just and the one who justifies those who have faith in Jesus" (ROMANS 3:26). Jesus' death was acceptable to God not because of who He was but because of what He was, "a lamb without blemish or defect" (1 PETER 1:19). "He did not enter by means of the blood of goats and calves; but he entered the Most Holy Place once for all by his own blood, having obtained eternal redemption" (HEBREWS 9:12). Christ became the ground on which God can "be just and the one who justifies those who have faith in Jesus" (ROMANS 3:26).

The New Testament declares that Jesus died for the world. When John the Baptist saw Jesus, he cried, "Look, the Lamb of God, who takes away the sin of the world!" (JOHN 1:29). Jesus said to Nicodemus, "For God so loved the world that he gave his one and only Son, that whoever believes in him shall not perish but have eternal life" (JOHN 3:16). Jesus said, "This bread is my flesh, which I will give for the life of the world" (JOHN 6:51). Paul wrote to the Corinthians that "God was reconciling the world to himself in Christ, not counting men's sins against them" (2 CORINTHIANS 5:19). John wrote, "And we have seen and testify that the Father has sent his Son to be the Savior of the world" (1 JOHN 4:14). "He is the atoning sacrifice for our sins, and not only for ours but also for the sins of the whole world" (1 JOHN 2:2).

The New Testament declares that Jesus died for all men and women. Jesus said, "I, when I am lifted up from the earth, will draw all men to myself" (JOHN 12:32). The apostle Paul wrote, "Consequently, just as the result of one trespass was condemnation for all men, so also the result of one act of righteousness was justification that brings life for all men" (ROMANS 5:18). He wrote to Timothy, "This is good, and pleases God our Savior, who wants all men to be saved and to come to a knowledge of the truth. For there is one God and one mediator between God and men, the man Christ Jesus, who gave himself as a ransom for all men—the testimony given in its proper time" (1 TIMOTHY 2:3–6). To Titus he wrote, "For the grace of God that brings salvation has appeared to all men" (TITUS 2:11 [RSV]).

Peter wrote, "But there were also false prophets among the people, just as there will be false teachers among you. They will secretly introduce destructive heresies, even denying the sovereign Lord who bought them" (2 PETER 2:1). The literal meaning is that Jesus paid their ransom, but they denied him! Paul makes it clear to Timothy that "(and for this we labor and strive), that we have put our hope in the living God, who is the Savior of all men, and especially of those who believe" (1 TIMOTHY 4:10).

Objectively, Jesus is the Savior of all men and women, but subjectively only those who believe are saved. Potentially, Jesus is the

Savior of all men and women, but effectively only those who believe experience salvation. The biblical truth of "a ransom for all men and women" brings worship, adoration, and praise to God, who is rich in mercy, great in love, and abundant in grace, not willing that any should perish but desiring that all should come to a knowledge of the truth!

Jesus Came to Give Life to Dead Men and Women

Jesus' death on the cross created the only way back to God, and that's why he came: to seek and to save the lost. We read this in JOHN 5:16–30. His great concern is not only to find the lost, but also to give life to dead men and women. He came that they might have life and have it to the full. He came to seek and save the lost, humans who were separated from God, but He also came to give life to dead humankind so that they could once more function and live correctly. His concern was not only restoring humankind to a right relationship with God, but also restoring humankind to right behavior. So He said, "I have come that they might have life" (JOHN 10:10).

Let me ask you this: Were the people that Jesus spoke to alive? Yes, they were alive—physically alive, but spiritually dead. "I have come that you might have life, and have it to the full," Jesus said (JOHN 10:10). That doesn't mean that you are going to be so busy you will die of busyness. It means that you are going to have a complete life, not just physically alive, not just soulishly alive, but spiritually alive.

Animals function by instinct. You can watch animals; for example, a hummingbird that builds a beautiful nest. Hummingbirds have been building the same nest for thousands of years. You never see a hummingbird building a three-deck nest with a screened-in porch. They just keep building the same way because they are pro-grammed by instinct to do it.

Salmon keep swimming up rivers and heading back to the same area they came from, century after century after century. They never stop and say, "Hey, how about going to the Canary Islands this time for the winter?" They go right straight back to Alaska. Are they crazy? No, they are programmed by instinct.

You and I were created to be indwelt by God. Because of Adam's fall, spiritually we are dead. Jesus said, "I have come that they might have life." He wants to come and take up residence with us so that

> *You and I were created to be indwelt by God. . . . He wants to come and take up residence with us . . . .*

His Spirit links with our spirit and becomes one Spirit, regenerating us, restoring us to life so that with our minds we can know Him, with our emotion we can feel Him, with our wills we can obey Him, and with our bodies we can serve Him and say, "Lord, here am I; use me." The Lord Jesus Christ came to give life to dead men and women, boys and girls. That is why He is called the Bread of Life (JOHN 6) and the Living Water (JOHN 4).

A hungry man needs bread to live. A thirsty man needs water to live. When you are dead spiritually, you need spiritual bread and spiritual water. Jesus said, "I am the living Bread" (JOHN 6:51), and "If you knew the gift of God and who it is that asks you for a drink, you would have asked him and he would have given you living water" (JOHN 4:10). He came not only to restore our relationship with God, through the cross, but to restore our behavior, by the resurrection, because He rose from the dead that He might come and live within us.

Listen to 1 CORINTHIAN 15:45: "the first man Adam became a living being; the last Adam, a life-giving Spirit." Jesus rose from the dead that He might give us His Spirit to live within us, so that where we are dead we might become alive.

That is why if someone is born into God's family, if they know the moment, hallelujah! If they can't precisely pinpoint that moment, but their lives are being conformed to the image of Jesus and evidence of the fruit of the Spirit is beginning to be displayed, do I have to

What is the essential fact?

The man who believes in

Him is not condemned.

chop these guys up, pull them down and knock them over and tell them, "You can't be saved because you can't tell me a moment"? Such a person knows there *was* a moment; he just can't touch on it. He can maybe narrow it down to a month or a week, and he says, "On Monday I did not believe, but on Friday I did believe." What is the essential fact? The man who believes in Him is not condemned. He who believes has eternal life. He who believes shall not perish. So this person has moved from unbelief to belief. I happen to remember the night I became a Christian and probably most of you also remember the moment when you became a Christian. The big question is not whether you can remember the exact moment, but rather whether your neighbors can see the life in you. That's the big question: Your neighbors, workmates, relations, friends—can they see the evidence of life?

How much more, having been reconciled, shall we be saved by His life! He rose from the dead that He might come and live within us. Jesus said, "Without me you can do nothing." But with the power of the risen Christ, I can do all things through Christ who strengthens me. Now Jesus, living within me as I put my faith in Him, restores me to a right relationship with God whereby I call Him Father. He rose from the dead and comes by His Spirit to live within me, taking up residence in my life so that I might be alive.

What is the evidence of death? Immorality, impurity, jealousy, greed, envy, murder, hate—sin. What is the evidence of life? Love, joy, peace, patience, kindness. It's not that you suddenly arrive, fully formed. Just because a baby is born physically doesn't mean that it is absolutely well trained and wonderfully adjusted to life and living in the neighborhood. That takes years. You know the baby is alive. You hope that one day it will get potty-trained and you hope it will learn that it can use a knife and a fork! You know the child is alive and you want and expect to see a progression. When you become alive, there is evidence of life, but there is room for growth and development and maturation. How much more, having been reconciled, shall we be saved by His life!

So Jesus said, "I have come that they might have life, and have it to the full" (JOHN 10:10). Not only this, but "I tell you the truth, whoever hears my words and believes him who sent me has eternal life and will not be condemned; he has crossed over from death to life" (JOHN 5:24). Understand this: The believer isn't going to get it, he already has it! He has eternal life and he will not be condemned, he has crossed over from death to life.

Now ask yourself, have you crossed over from death to life? Is there evidence in your life—in the way you live, the way you behave —indicating that you have crossed over from death to life? As someone well said, you don't have to ram religion down people's throats,

> *Is there evidence in your life ... indicating that you have crossed over from death to life?*

you just need to let God loose in your life and people will see that your life is different. What you do need to communicate to them is how you became different, and how they can become different. It is no use trying to convince people if there is no evidence of life, because actions speak louder than words.

"I tell you the truth, whoever hears my words and believes him who sent me has eternal life and will not be condemned; he has crossed over from death to life" (JOHN 5:24). "As in Adam all die, so in

Christ all are made alive" (1 CORINTHIANS 15:22). When I become a member of the body of Christ, I put my faith in the Lord Jesus Christ. Where once I was in darkness, now I am in light. Where once I was dead, now I am alive. Where once I was in sinking sands, now I am on solid rock. I am a member of His body, His family. No longer dead in Adam, I am alive in Jesus.

That is what the resurrection is all about. It is the person of the risen Christ coming to take up residence within you so that where you were malfunctioning you might begin to function correctly; where you were living wrongly, you might begin to live correctly. The promise of God's Word is that when we cross over from death to life, there is now no condemnation, and in Christ all are made alive. There is also the wondrous truth of ROMANS 8:2: "Through Christ Jesus the law of the Spirit of life sets me free from the law of sin and death."

I suppose one of the hardest things I grappled with was this concept that when you become a Christian you are no longer under law. I found that hard to grasp. I can remember going back to Bible school and talking to the chairman of the Theology Department at Moody Bible Institute, Fred Dickinson, and saying to him, "Can you explain to me again how I am not under law but have to be lawful?" I had been away from school for five years. "Can you explain to me again how I am not under law and yet I have got to be lawful?" Now, I am sure he did a good job of teaching, but I just didn't see it. I struggled with it. I could not grasp it. One illustration, which I first heard used by my former pastor, Alan Redpath, has helped immensely and I never move away from that illustration. Here it is.

It is not just hearing it [the truth], it is grasping it and then beginning to believe and letting it loose in your life. Note ROMANS 8:2: "Through Christ Jesus the law of the Spirit of life sets me free from the law of sin and death." You will notice that God's law never made anyone perfect—did you notice that? It just showed you that you weren't perfect. Yet when I became a Christian, I am no longer under that old law of sin and death. I am under a new law, the law of the Spirit of life in Christ Jesus, which means that when I allow Him to live in me and through me, He will produce through me a life-style that will in fact keep the law, without me even thinking about it!

I got on a flight from London Heathrow to Chicago. It was a jumbo 747 and I boarded with about 250 other people. As the passengers got on, no one asked the cabin crew, "By the way, how do you get this big bird off the ground?" They got on, sat in their seats, and then did everything they were told. Would you please stow your tables, put your seats to an upright position, fasten your seat belts, and prepare for takeoff? It is amazing, everyone does it. Click, click. Then the plane moves out to the end of the runway and you hear the captain saying, "Flight attendants, please take your seats and prepare for takeoff." Everything goes quite quiet, with no one shouting, "Hey, hold it a minute! Gravity says this thing can't get off the ground!" Everyone sits there. Then you hear the big engines beginning to rev, and the plane begins to move slowly along the runway. It is interesting: even halfway along the runway it is moving pretty fast, and a whole stack of people are convinced it should be off the ground by then and lift their feet to help it! By three-quarters of the way along the runway, it is really moving, and all the Christians are now praying as they never prayed before. Isn't that right? They begin to say, "Lord, I will never be nasty to my wife again—just get this plane up." They commit themselves to missionary service in Greenland! "I'll go to Greenland, Lord, just get this plane up!" They make up for the whole year of prayer that they have missed all in one moment, even though the plane is still not up. Then, finally, it begins to lift.

All I know is that gravity says it is not allowed off the ground, so why is it taking off? What has happened to gravity? Has it stopped? No, gravity is still trying to pull the plane down, but a whole new law has come into effect. It is the law of aerodynamics, and the plane is now meeting the requirements of this new law, which doesn't do away with the old law of gravity, it only supersedes the old law. As long as the plane meets the requirements of the new law, it will continue to supersede the old law that is still trying to pull it down, and it will fly. The moment it fails to meet the requirements of the new law, guess what? The old law will immediately take over and the plane will crash.

When you and I became Christians, the Holy Spirit of the risen Christ came to live within us. As long as we meet the requirements of the new law, walking in the Spirit, the old law, the lust of the flesh, which seeks to pull us down and cause us to sin, cannot do it because it is superseded by the new law! The moment we stop meeting the requirements of this new law and stop walking in the Spirit, the old lust-of-the-flesh law takes over and we crash and commit sin. You see, the old law is not done away with, it is just superseded. As long as I walk in the Spirit, I do not fulfill the lusts of the flesh, but the moment I stop walking in the Spirit, the lusts of the flesh will take over and I will crash, I will sin.

'The entire law is summed up in a single command: "Love your neighbor as yourself" (GALATIANS 5:14). If I allow the Spirit of the risen Christ to control my life, He will produce through me what I can't produce by myself: the fruit of the Spirit. So, when I am controlled by the Spirit, He will produce through me the fruit of the Spirit, which is love—and if I love my neighbor, guess what? I will not lie to him. I automatically keep the law without even thinking about it. If I love my neighbor, I will not steal from him, so I automatically keep the law without thinking about it. If I love my neighbor, I will not commit adultery with his wife, so I automatically keep the law without even thinking about it. I don't have to think about the law. What I have to think about is walking in the power of the risen Christ. The positive handles the negative. The Light handles the darkness. The life handles the death!

Too many people, as Christians, try to live by their own efforts and go around thinking, "I mustn't steal, I mustn't steal, it looks good! I must not look lustfully, oh, I mustn't look lustfully, I mustn't." That is not the way to truly live. You can't do it by yourself. The issue is that I must abide in Christ. I must walk in the Light. I must walk in the Spirit. I must meet the requirements of this new law. I must make myself available as a living sacrifice. I must have my mind renewed. I must have my mind filled with God's truth and principles. I must live by faith. As I do, the risen Christ, living within me by His Spirit, makes me strong where I am weak; where I am wrong, He makes me right. All because He rose from the dead and He is alive in my life.

That is what Christianity is all about. Don't get me wrong, but isn't that a lot better than thinking you are going to heaven and having a hell of the time getting there? Isn't it? Christ living in you means that you are still going to heaven, but you are having a heavenly time getting there! Oh, it doesn't do away with pressures and problems, the storms and the dark valleys, but you have never seen a beautiful valley until you have been on a high mountain, and you have never seen a beautiful mountain till you have walked in a low valley. You need the mountains and the valleys, and the God of the mountains and the valleys wants to walk hand-in-hand with you through both.

This is what makes Christianity exciting to me ... that I have come to the cross ....

This is what makes Christianity exciting to me. It simply means that I have come to the cross, I have put my faith in Jesus, and I have been reconciled to God and He is my Father. I am back in the relationship that Adam lost, walking hand-in-hand with God. The Jesus who rose from the dead has come to live within me to restore me to life, so that I can actually become the man, the husband, the father I was created to be. Without Him, it is impossible. On top of that, one day I shall see Him and be like Him!

Humankind was created in the image of God: an image of holiness that provided the freedom for fellowship, and an image of personality that provided the capacity for fellowship. The wonderful truth was that Adam walked and talked with God. God said, "The day you disobey me you will die"; man disobeyed, and he died in his relationship with God and in his behavior, so that he no longer reflected the likeness of God. Instead of being in a right relationship with God, he was separated and out of contact with God. Instead of reflecting the likeness of the God who had made him, he began to reflect his own likeness, his deadness and his sinfulness. That is the simple statement the Bible makes: Humankind is dead in sin. On that basis, the need is to get him alive again, restore him to life in the areas in which he is dead. He needs to come alive in his relationship to God and he needs to come alive like God in his behavior.

God is the only one who can do anything about that need. You cannot regenerate yourself when you are dead. You cannot restore that relationship; you do not have the ability or the power to do it. That is why God sent his Son, the God-man, the Lord Jesus Christ, to die on the cross: so that we might be reconciled to God. That takes care of the problem of separation. Jesus rose from the dead to come and live within us, and that takes care of the problem of malfunctioning, our inability to behave correctly. You see, a Christian is a person who is in a right relationship to God by faith in the Lord Jesus Christ. He is a person who is reflecting the likeness of God through the power of the indwelling Spirit of the Lord Jesus Christ.

ROMANS 5:10 says: "When we were God's enemies, we were reconciled to him through the death of his Son, how much more, having been reconciled, shall we be saved through his life!" Jesus said that He came to seek and to save the lost. Jesus came to give life to dead men and women. The Lord Jesus Christ has done everything, absolutely everything, to enable you and to enable me to have a right relationship with God and to begin once more to reflect the likeness of God. God is our Father, so his children should reflect the family likeness!

The Cross, the Resurrection

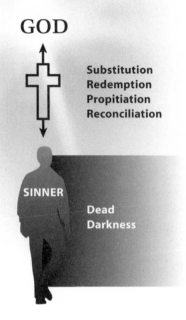

For the son of Man came to seek and to save what was lost.

—LUKE 19:10

I have come that they may have life and have it to the full.

—JOHN 10:10b

THE NEW MAN

4

The New Man's Position Is in Christ

1 CORINTHIANS 15:22 deals with man's new position in Christ: "For as in Adam all die, so in Christ all will be made alive." Here is an important fact. Adam's children bear the likeness of Adam. Adam lost his relationship with God, lost his ability to behave and function correctly, and his children were born in his likeness. God's children, born into His family, have the ability to behave and function correctly bearing His likeness. We have to ask ourselves, how do we get out of Adam, in whom all people are dead, and into the body of Christ, where all people are made alive? In Adam all die; that is, they are disconnected from God. In Christ all are made alive; that is, reconnected to God.

There are those who are dead in Adam and those who are alive in Jesus. Without being unfair or unkind, there is no way you can tell who is who by looking at a person's face. It is totally impossible. People sometimes say, "Oh, he or she has a lovely Christian smile." I am not so sure; sometimes that expression may appear just because they like pecan ice cream! You have always got to be careful when you look at people's expressions and call them Christlike or Christian. In the end, the important point to remember is that we are either dead in Adam or we are alive in Jesus. The longer you know someone, the more aware you should be of what position he or she is in. If a person bears the likeness of death, then his or her life will be marked with immorality or impurity or greed or jealousy or envy or murder or hate, or a combination. In contrast, if a person bears the likeness of life, he or she will be growing in the new relationship of being alive in Christ. These people will be reflecting the likeness of God through their lives as the fruit of Spirit is being produced: love or joy or peace or patience or kindness, or a combination.

There shouldn't be too much difficulty, after a while, in discovering to which family an individual belongs, Adam's family of death or Jesus' family of life. Our question is, if I come and put my faith in the Lord Jesus who died for me, and He becomes my Lord and Savior, how do I get out of Adam and into the body of Christ?

In Adam all die, in Christ all are made alive. "For we were all baptized by one Spirit into one body—whether Jews or Greeks, slaves or free—and we were all given the one Spirit to drink" (1 CORINTHIANS 12:13). I know, and some of you know and realize, that this is a fascinating verse. Paul's letter to the Corinthians is a corrective epistle. He is not writing a nasty-gram, he is writing a corrective letter to help them. Over and over again, in different ways, he tells them that they are not all this and they are not all that. For instance, in that very same chapter, he asks the rhetorical question: "Are all apostles?" Paul is not writing to a bunch of carnal Christians, saying, "By the way, can you maybe give me a little help, I am wondering if everyone is an apostle?" No, he is using a teaching device, the rhetorical question, and he asks, in almost staccato fashion, question after question. Are all apostles?

Are all prophets? Are all workers of miracles? Do all speak in tongues? Do all interpret? Do all this, do all that? The answer keeps coming back like an echo: No! No!! No!!!

Yet in that same chapter he has already said, "For we were all baptized by one Spirit into one body—whether Jews or Greeks, slaves or free." What is he saying? He is saying this. When you put your faith in the Lord Jesus Christ, the Holy Spirit took you out of the body of Adam in which you were dead, separated from God, and placed you into the body of Christ where you became alive, reconnected to God. You became a member of Christ's body, of which He is the head. He gives gifts to the members of the body to enable the body to operate, function, and be healthy.

Think of your own body. There are many parts of the body that can do nothing for themselves. Therefore, hands are helpful. You can have itches in annoying places that only the hands can reach. You can wash toes with hands; you don't wash toes with your other foot.

You can adapt, though. Once I was in a car on the Isle of Man. The young man driving it had no arms, so he did everything with his feet. He was brilliant and I was amazed. The first thing I wanted to know was where he put the car key. The next minute he kicks his shoe off and takes out the key that was in his shoe. He had been walking on it all the time! Up comes his foot holding the key with his toes, unlocks the door, opens it, and he gets in! It was incredible. I was in college and all the students saw me going out with him. It was interesting, they all wanted to see how he was going to drive the car. It was even more interesting sitting beside him!

Though hands are very helpful, they're not enough by themselves alone. Your hand is wonderful, but it cannot scratch its own back. It needs the other hand to do that. Hands are helpful for putting food into your mouth, but the mouth is wonderful at dealing with the food! It doesn't give it back to the hand and say, "You chew for a while." All the different parts of the body are necessary because each part functions to help the whole body operate correctly.

So it is within God's family, the body of Christ. He has given us gifts so that we might minister to one another and so that collectively we will be healthy. We are to operate in harmony with the head. That is the most important job.

Here is another point, now that you are no longer dead in Adam, but are alive in Christ. The Spirit of God has placed you in the body of Christ. 2 CORINTHIANS 5:17 says: "If anyone be in Christ, he is a new creation; The old has gone, the new has come." Now, note the words "in Christ." In Adam all die, in Christ all are made alive. For by one Spirit we were all baptized into one body. Therefore, if anyone be in Christ, he is a new person. It's not your membership in the church that is important. It's your membership in the body of Christ that is important. Membership in a church doesn't mean that you are a member of the body of Christ. When you and I put our faith in the Lord Jesus, the Holy Spirit placed us into the body of Christ. If anyone be in Christ, he is a new person. So ask yourself, "Am I in Christ or am I not?" If you are in Christ, you are a new person. The old, dead in Adam, has gone; the new, in Christ, has come!

I know that many people who become Christians somehow or other expect everything to become new. They expect to wake up in the morning and see the seagulls doing somersaults. Well, it doesn't happen that way. It is the old that has gone. What was the old? Dead in sin. What is new? You are alive in Christ. Old was in darkness; now the new you is in the light. The old, broad road led to destruction; the new you is on a narrow road that leads to life. The old was in sinking sands; the new you is standing on solid rock. The old child of the devil has gone; the new has come, now you are a child of God. Hallelujah!

We belong; we are His children. We are in His family. If anyone be in Christ, he is a new person. So we have a new position: We are members in the body of Christ. He is the head, and He gives gifts to the body that we might minister to one another to help one another. Not only do we have this new position in Christ, but we also have this wonderful experience that He is in us. He, the Lord Jesus Christ, is in us!

The New Man's Practice Is Christ in the Believer

A key passage is COLOSSIANS 1:27: "To them God has chosen to make known among the Gentiles the glorious riches of this mystery, which is Christ in you, the hope of Glory." Now that is really quite a mouthful. Let me try to break it down.

"To them God has chosen to make known among the Gentiles the glorious riches of this mystery"—what mystery? A *mystery*, in the New Testament, was something that had not been revealed in the Old Testament and now is being made known. What was this mystery? This mystery was "Christ in you, the hope of Glory." The word *hope* in the Bible never means wishful thinking. We use it that way in Scotland when we say we hope it is going to be a nice day tomorrow. That is wishful thinking! Hope? I hope I am going to get a big present for Christmas; for some kids, that is just wishful thinking. Or the woman who says, "I hope I am going to get that diamond" — wishful thinking! I hope, I hope . . . there are loads of wishful thinking.

> *... I have been telling you*
>
> *that glory isn't heaven. . . .*
>
> *Glory is the reflected*
>
> *likeness of God himself.*

In the Bible, though, the word *hope* has the connotation of confidence. So Paul is saying Christ in you, the confidence of glory. But I have been telling you that glory isn't heaven. Heaven will be glorious because Christ is there, but heaven isn't the point. What did I suggest that *glory* meant? Glory is the reflected likeness of God himself.

Here's the mystery: Christ in you, the confidence of the reflected likeness of God. Without Jesus in you, you can have no confidence that you can reflect the likeness of God—it is totally impossible. It is as impossible as for a car with no gas to drive off down the road. But with Christ in you, you have the confidence that you, now— not then or one day, but now—can begin to reflect the likeness of God. He is the source and power to accomplish this and He is our confidence. For Jesus said, "Without me you can do nothing," but with Him living within me, I can do all things through Christ who strengthens me!

The wonderful truth is this. Now, with Jesus living in my life, by His Spirit, I can have the confidence of beginning to reflect the likeness of God, and becoming the person I was created to be. That is the wonder. Many people say, "I will never be able to keep it up." Do you know what God says? That's absolutely right. You will not.

I remember a speech by Major Ian Thomas, given at the British Evangelists' Conference, which I attended more than thirty years ago. "Do you know what God expects of you? He only expects one thing of you." I thought, what is it going to be?

God expects nothing from you or from me except total failure.

Then he said: "Total failure." I know what he means, and it is true. God expects nothing from you or from me except total failure. That's why He raised Jesus from the dead to come and live within me, because without Him we can do nothing; we are total failures. But in the power of the risen Christ I can do all things, through Christ who strengthens me. The potential is there. That is where our confidence lies, "Christ in you, the hope of Glory." He has come to live within us to enable us to reflect the likeness of God. Now, with God in our lives we can be godly, with Christ in our lives we can be Christ-like, and with the Holy Spirit in our lives we can produce the fruit of the Spirit!

Let me propose something to you. You are body and you are soul/spirit. I am not a dichotomist or a trichotomist; I am in between. I don't think there is a true division between soul and spirit. I believe there is an interlacing, an interlocking. You have got a body. I can't see the real you; I can only see your body. (If I could, no doubt you would all look good!) You can't do anything without your body. You have to do everything with your body. At the end of the day, if you want to put your thoughts into action, you have to do it with your body. If you want to play a ball game, you have to take your body and play it. If you want to go fishing, your body has got to go as well. If you want to go to work, your body has to go to work. If you want to eat, your body has to eat. That also applies in the area of sexuality. You cannot do anything without your body. It is so important. We carry and take it everywhere we go.

But your body isn't the real you. Oh yes, that is you, but it's not the *real* you. One day that body will just die. It will be gone, like an old tent. The you that lived in the tent will leave. Living within that body is a soul/spirit. You can break that soulishness down to very similar relationships to your personality: mind, emotion, and will. What do you do if you are not a Christian and your mind is darkened? What do you do if your emotion is debased? What do you do if your will is bent toward evil? Well, if you really want to be good or improve, you will do everything you can to discipline yourself. Discipline your mind, feed the mind; control these emotions of anger and rage with anger management classes; try and control your will. In the end, you will discover that you've still got problems.

The spirit within man is dead because the life of God left him, and man's spirit can be alive only when the very life of God is within man's spirit. That's why, when someone becomes a Christian, a wonderful thing takes place. The Spirit of the risen Christ comes to live within the spirit of man. The Bible says, "But he who unites himself with the Lord is one with him in spirit" (1 CORINTHIANS 6:17). We need the Spirit of God in our lives to regenerate and restore our spirits and bring them back to life.

With the Spirit having restored our spirits to life, now we can know the truth in our minds, and that truth will set us free. Now we can know the power of Christ within our emotions as we express ourselves. We can yield ourselves to His will so that we live in obedience to His will. Sin is when we turn to God and say, "Hang it, I am not going to pay any attention. I am going to do it my way. I will run my own life. You will not tell me what to do."

We were created to say, "Not my will, but Your will."

We were created to say, "Not my will, but Your will." We need to submit to His will. As He lives within us, we have a restored spirit; we have a mind that we might know Him, emotion that we might feel

Him, and a will that we might obey Him. We give our bodies as a living sacrifice and say, "Lord, here am I; use me."

I was asked to speak at chapel at Moody Bible Institute on knowing God's will. I think they really wanted me to say that if you truly want God's will, you will end up as a pastor or a missionary. I heard a well-known pastor say that the greatest calling of all is the calling of a pastor. Do you know what that implies? That no one else can have quite the same level of calling. I don't agree with that, because God calls everyone to ministry that is essential for the body. The important thing is not the ministry, the important thing is the person who makes it possible. The important thing is not the gift, it is the giver. We are all needed to bring Him glory. Man's chief end is to glorify God and to enjoy Him forever. I shared some of this truth at the Institute.

It makes no difference whether you are cleaning the streets or serving on a mission field. The important thing is presenting your body as a living sacrifice and saying, "Lord, here am I; use me." You

> *The important thing is presenting your body as a living sacrifice and saying, "Lord, here am I; use me."*

don't hear of too many pastors who were around at the feeding of the five thousand, but you do know there was a little boy there with five loaves and two sardines. He made himself available and said, "Here am I; use me." You don't hear of too many preachers who were around when Goliath was taken on by the children of Israel, but you do know there was a little boy with one sling and five stones. So, day by day, whether you are working in an office, whether you are working in the kitchen, whether you are working at school, whether you are outdoors or indoors, whether you have got an important job or an unimportant job, the important thing is to say, "Lord, here I am; use me."

Fulfillment isn't reaching the top of the ladder. I heard a preacher say that some people get to the top of the ladder only to discover that it is leaning against the wrong building, and that's horrifying! The important thing is being who God created you to be: you. That is fulfillment. I would say that what has excited me most is just being me.

When I was growing up, I used to have people say to me, "Why can't you stop talking so much? Why don't you stop talking so much?" I remember going to a party and saying to myself, "All right, I am going to keep my mouth shut. I will show them I can keep my mouth shut." I sat at that party and said nothing. Guess what they were saying to me after five minutes? "What's wrong with you tonight?" You can't win.

A girl came up to me at Moody Bible Institute after I had spoken at chapel and said, "I have got a problem similar to you." Boy, was I interested to know her problem! She said, "I have got a big mouth." (She nearly had a bigger one!) I remember saying to her that the important thing is not the size of your mouth, but making your mouth available to God so He can channel it to His glory. That is what is important.

"Christ in you, the hope of Glory." Now, with Christ living within me, I can give Him my mind and say, "Lord, here is my mind to think through." I can give Him my emotions and say, "Lord, here is my emotion to feel through." I can give Him my will and say, "Lord, here is my will to act through." I can give Him my body and say, "Lord, here is my body to live through." It doesn't matter where I am, who I am, or what I am, as long as I am making myself available for the glory of God. He wants to take the ordinary to do the extraordinary. That's exciting.

When I was in my teens, I listened to Billy Graham regularly on Radio Luxembourg, 11:30 on Wednesday nights. I used to memorize everything. I used to hear Cliff Barrows come on and I memorized what he said: "This is the Hour of Decision brought to you transcribed by the Billy Graham Broadcasting Association. This is Cliff Barrows speaking on behalf of Mr. Graham and the whole team." I knew it by heart. Thursday night was: "This is the Old Fashioned Revival Hour, coming to you from the Municipal Auditorium, Long Beach, California." I used to know that by heart, too. This was followed by Rudy Atwood playing "Heavenly Sunshine." After I heard it on the radio on Wednesday, I used to preach Billy Graham's sermon the following week at the open-air service at The Mound, Edinburgh.

In 1955, I went to hear Billy Graham at the Kelvin Hall, in Glasgow, Scotland. The first thing I discovered was that there were 12,000 people there, which was a bit more than the hundred who attended my church. Here was this man up front conducting, Cliff Barrows. I was mesmerized, because the church I attended didn't even use any musical instruments. I thought, "My goodness me, I will have to learn to conduct like him," and I'd swing my hands up and down, back and over, until I could do it exactly as he did. I used to practice in front of the mirror until I could do it exactly like Cliff Barrows; always with the cuffs up when you put on the jacket. I thought, "Now when Cliff Barrows dies, Billy will phone me and say, 'Ian, I need you!'" You know, Cliff Barrows is still living; he was with Billy Graham for their last crusade in New York in 2006!

Ah, but the next item that came along was George Beverley Shea. I had never heard soloists before, because we didn't have soloists in our church. (We did, however, have a man who always sang louder than the others!) I thought, "I have got to sing like Bev Shea." I remember that the first 78 record I ever got was George Beverley Shea singing "How Great Thou Art." I copied it onto a reel-to-reel tape so I could sing a duet with Bev Shea, singing along with the tape. How many of you have a tape of singing with Bev Shea? You guessed it. Then along came Billy Graham to preach. Man, I wanted to preach like Billy Graham, so every Saturday night I used to preach the Wednesday-night sermon of Billy Graham on the Hour of Decision on Radio Luxembourg in the open air at The Mound in Edinburgh. I was a sixteen-year-old boy, preaching someone else's words and using illustrations about people I didn't even know.

Do you know what I was doing all that time? Destroying me being me. God didn't create me to be Cliff Barrows. God didn't create me to be Bev Shea. God didn't create me to be Billy Graham. He created me to be Ian Leitch. One thing that will frustrate you more than any other is trying to be someone else. Oh, you certainly can learn from other people. I have learned, and am still learning, from other people. I watch and I observe and I listen, and when I see good points I want to learn from them so that I can be a better Ian Leitch and fulfill myself. The moment I try to imitate someone else, though, I am absolutely in trouble. I began to discover that Christ in me, the confidence of reflected likeness, is simply that He lives within not to destroy me but to make me who He created me to be. That takes off a lot of pressure. There is no competition, there is just the need to be me.

In ROMANS 8:9–10 we read: "You, however, are not controlled by the sinful nature but the Spirit, if the Spirit of God lives in you. And if anyone does not have the Spirit of Christ, He does not belong to Christ." Two things to observe. Here is the great demarcation between the believer and the nonbeliever, the Christian and the non-Christian. The Christian has the Spirit of the risen Christ living within him, who restores him to life. He does not have the Spirit who does not belong to Him, and he remains dead. If the Spirit of God lives in you, what happens? It starts at the beginning of the verse. "You, however, are not controlled by the sinful nature but by the Spirit if the Spirit of God lives in you." He has come to take up residence in our lives. He is the controller of your life to enable you to live in harmony with the Word of God and be open to the will of God, so that you might be what God wants you to be—a person who reflects His likeness.

There was a saying at Moody when I was a student which indicated that many people thought Moody was a sausage machine:

It was just pushing out Christian sausages, all looking the same, behaving the same, acting the same. I began to meditate and think about that. I don't know how you buy sausages in the United States. In Scotland, if you get them all linked together, you ask for one pound or two pounds of sausages from the person who cuts them. You don't go to the butcher and say, "By the way, I want one or two sausages. I'll take that one there; oh, I love the shape of that one. That's a cute one there. I would like this one over here, I really like the style, that one has got pizzazz. Give me this one here, it's a cute little freaky thing." You just order a pound of sausages because they all come out basically the same.

> *Every Christian is indwelt by Christ, but every Christian expresses Christlikeness in many different ways ....*

God doesn't operate a sausage machine. Guess what He operates? A snowblower. (No, I don't mean that we're all flaky!) He operates a snowblower in which every flake is different but every flake is snow. Every Christian is indwelt by Christ, but every Christian expresses Christlikeness in many different ways according to their temperaments. That is wonderful. He wants you to be you. He wants to control you so that He can produce through your life the fruit of the Spirit, using your temperament, your abilities, your talents so that He may be seen a hundred thousand different ways of Christ-likeness.

Christ in me, the hope, the confidence of reflected likeness. "But if Christ is in you, your body is dead because of sin, yet your spirit is alive because of righteousness" (ROMANS 8:10). "And if the Spirit of Him who raised Jesus from the dead is living in you, He who raised Christ from the dead will also give life to your mortal bodies through his Spirit, who lives in you" (ROMANS 8:11). So the wonderful truth is that the Spirit who raised Jesus from the dead is the Spirit that lives within you to give you victory and power over sin, that you might live in such a way that you reflect the likeness of the God who made you.

It would be foolish for us all to try to be the same, because we all have different temperaments. Say you came to Edinburgh to watch a rugby game between Scotland and England at Murrayfield Stadium. It's called "the battle of the old enemies." Make no mistake, when they go out to play each other, it is not a nice little game; they are hitting each other hard and it is a brawl in many ways. There's an interesting demonstration, at each game, of the four basic temperaments: sanguine, choleric, phlegmatic, and melancholic. Each crowd has amazing mixes of each. When Scotland scores a try, you just need to turn round and you will see hundreds of Scotsmen wearing kilts, ten feet in the air — don't use your imagination too much — throwing their hands in the air.

They are known as sanguine because when England scores, these same people who were ten feet in the air are now ten feet under the ground in despair!

There is also the choleric. When Scotland scores, he is the man who analyzes the game specifically and says, "Well done, Scotland, well done, now let's consolidate our position with another score." When England scores, he doesn't go ten feet underground. He just says, "All right, Scotland, one try, that's all right, let's regroup, let's rethink, let's get back into the battle, the game's not over yet, we can make it." He is a handy person to have around when the pressure is on.

Oh, but when Scotland scores there's also the phlegmatic who is never up and never down, he is just blah. You turn round and say to him, "Scotland scored," and he says, "I know, I saw it." And when England scores you say, "England scored," and he says, "I know, I saw it." He is the sort of person who, when an earthquake hits, says, "Yes, I know, I was there." That is all he will say. I have had more mothers complain about their phlegmatic teenage daughters than any other temperament. They cannot stand these daughters who are neither up nor down. I remember phoning a family I know well and got the phlegmatic daughter on the line. I was calling from Scotland; she was living in the USA. I said, "Hey, this is Ian."

"Hello."

I said, "I am calling from Scotland."

"Yeh."

"Are your mom and dad home?"

"No."

"Could you take a message?"

"I guess."

"I am coming in tomorrow, could you ask your mum and dad to pick me up at 5:30 and if they can't make it, no problem."

"OK."

"See you tomorrow."

"Bye."

Want to know something? She was meant to be excited, but you could have fooled me. If I had phoned and told her that half of Scotland had sunk and everyone had drowned, she would have said the same thing: "Really." So Scotland scores: "I saw it"; England scores: "I saw it."

There is still one temperament left, the melancholic. When Scotland scores, the sanguine is up in the air; the choleric is clapping his hands saying, "Let's consolidate"; the phlegmatic is saying, "I know, I saw it"; and the melancholic is saying, in a weepy voice, that one try is not enough, oh we need more, we definitely, oh, we definitely need more. Melancholics are the only ones who can cry over good news! When England scores, they say, "I told you we needed more." Have you met people like that? My mother was a classic melancholic.

Can you pick yourself out of these descriptions? Can you pick out some of your temperaments? You see it is important. Why?

You don't want a surgeon to be a sanguine. You don't want him poking around and shouting, "Look what I found in here! Man, I've got his kidneys, ha ha ha." Then, "Oh my, I can't get them back in again." You don't want that sort of guy handling you. In contrast, you don't want a phlegmatic greeting people at the door of the church.

God created man in His image, an image of holiness and an image of personality. Holiness provided the freedom for fellowship and personality provided the capacity or the ability for fellowship, with the wonderful results that man walked and talked with God. God created man to walk hand-in-hand with Him, but God also said, "The day you disobey me, you die." Man disobeyed God and he died. He died in the areas in which he had been alive. He had been alive in his relationship with God and he died in his relationship with God. He lost that relationship. Death is separation. God the Creator and man the creature no longer walked hand-in-hand. Man also died in his ability to reflect the likeness of God, his Creator, and he began to reveal his own inadequacy, his own sin, his own death, because the evidence of death is immorality, impurity, greed, jealousy, envy, murder, hate, and so on, while the evidence of life is love, joy, peace, patience, kindness, goodness, gentleness, meekness, self-control. The Bible simply says that man's basic problem is that he is dead in sin and he is walking in darkness.

God, who saw man in his need, took the initiative and decided to help man. He sent His Son, the God-man, into this world. The Lord Jesus Christ came into the world and said, "I have come to seek and to save the lost." He came to seek and save lost men and women, people out of contact with God, so that they might be restored into a living relationship with God. Jesus also said, "I have come that they might have life": so that dead men and women, boys and girls, who are malfunctioning, behaving incorrectly, might be indwelt by the risen Christ and once more begin to live and behave correctly. In other words, so that they might once more reflect the likeness of the God who made them; that they might glorify, reflect, the likeness of God.

Salvation is found in Jesus alone. We are reconciled to God through the death of His Son, and we are made alive by His life. He died on the cross to reconnect us and He rose from the dead to regenerate us to behave correctly. When you and I put our faith in the Lord Jesus, we were reconciled to God. God was in Christ reconciling the world to Himself, making a way back. When you put your faith in Him, you are reconciled to God, you are restored to the relationship Adam lost. Jesus also rose from the dead, and when we put our faith in Him, the Lord Jesus who rose from the dead, by His Spirit, comes to live within us and is united to our spirit; becoming one spirit, He regenerates, restores us to life again so that we can reflect the likeness of God.

This involves two things. The Bible says, "In Adam all die, in Christ all will be made alive." When I put my faith in Jesus, I am taken out of Adam and placed into the body of Christ as an individual member, and given gifts that under the leadership of the Head I might minister to the needs of the body so that the body might operate and behave correctly in relationship to the Head, each ministering to one another with the gifts that God has given, not for our self-enjoyment but for the edification of the body. If anyone be in Christ, he is a new person.

Not only is it true that we are in Christ, but there is also the wonderful truth that Christ is in us. We saw that the Holy Spirit comes to take up residence within our spirit, becomes one spirit with our spirit so that now we have the life source, the power source—"without me you can do nothing"—to think correctly with our minds, feel correctly with our emotions, decide correctly with our wills, and live correctly with our bodies. He comes in to give us what we lack. Christ in you, the hope of—what does the word *hope* mean?—the confidence of glory. What does *glory* mean? Reflected likeness. When Christ is within me, I have the confidence to be the person He created me to be. Not someone else, though I can learn from others. Not imitating someone else, though it can be helpful to watch how they live. It means allowing the risen Christ to so live in me that I am fulfilled as me and I become the person God created me to be and the person I long to be.

Restored Relationship, Restored Behavior

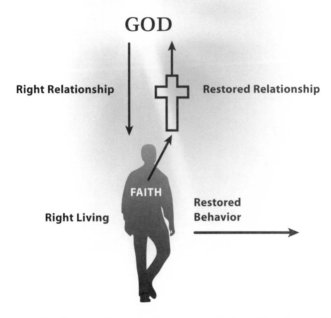

When we were God's enemies, we were reconciled to him through the death of his Son, how much more, having been reconciled, shall we be saved through his life!

—ROMANS 5:10

THE SPIRITUAL PERSON

We now move on to the spiritual man, as described in 1 CORINTHIANS 2. In verse 14, Paul talks about the natural man, the nonbeliever, as not having the Spirit and not accepting the things that come from God. The man without the Spirit does not accept the things that come from the Spirit of God. Have you ever noticed that with your friends who aren't Christians? When they don't have the Holy Spirit, they don't even begin to understand, or grasp, what you are talking about. They don't understand the things that come from the Spirit of God. Many a time they are not even sympathetic, for such ideas and experiences are foolishness to them; they cannot understand these things because they are spiritually dead.

In chapter 3, verses 1–4, Paul describes carnal Christians as mere infants in Christ. They are still on milk, not solid food; they are still worldly, not spiritual; they are acting as mere men (that is, unbelievers). Then there is the spiritual Christian. I want to look at what Paul says concerning the spiritual man in 1 CORINTHIANS 2. Verse 15 says, "The spiritual man makes judgments about all things, but he himself is not subject to any man's judgment: 'For who has known the mind of the Lord that He may instruct him?' But we have the mind of Christ," that is, the spiritual man does. "Brothers, I could not address you as spiritual but as worldly—mere infants in Christ. I gave you milk, not solid food, for you were not yet ready for it. Indeed you are still not ready. You are still worldly. For since there is jealousy and quarrelling among you, are you not worldly? Are you not acting like mere men? For when one says, 'I follow Paul,' and another, 'I follow Apollos,' are you not mere men?"

The issue here is spirituality. You see, God wants us to become mature spiritually. You cannot be spiritual without the Holy Spirit, you cannot be Christlike without the Lord Jesus Christ, and you cannot be godly without God. The fact that Christ lives in us by His Spirit means that we are alive and traveling down the right road. We are in the right family. However, children have to grow, develop, and mature, and we all do this in different stages and at different rates. We find the same within God's family. God's concern is that we might be conformed to His image. His concern is that we are being conformed now, being changed from glory to glory; changed from reflected likeness to reflected likeness until one day we will see Him and be like Him.

After I preached in Johnston, Scotland, a twenty-year-old said to me, "You are a lot better than when I heard you four years ago." That's what you call straight and to the point! I said that I hoped I was, and that I hoped it was more than just my preaching: I hoped I was better spiritually as well. I hope that if you come back in four years and hear me again that you will be able to say the same thing. Wouldn't it be dreadful if, after four years, the person said, "You are no better than you were the last time." There has to be growth. There has to be development. There has to be maturation.

The tragedy is that our age spiritually isn't always equal to our growth spiritually. Just think for a moment about when you became a Christian. For some people, that was more than ten years ago. For some, it was more than twenty years ago. For me, it was more than fifty-five years ago, and I have to confess that there is no way I am fifty-five years spiritually mature. So, if you have been saved for five years, are you five years spiritually mature? Have you grown and matured as you should?

What we find is that, just as in any other areas of life, we can be fifty years of age but not have developed our mental ability to the maturity or level that a fifty-year-old should have. Most of us have not. Have we developed our bodies? Most of us have destroyed them! It is the same spiritually.

God's concern is that we grow spiritually, really at the same rate as we are growing age-wise. That is His desire: that day by day we are growing and developing into mature Christians. There are times when we may experience sudden "growth spurts" in our spiritual lives. I know that I have been at conferences, or I have listened to a preacher, and suddenly everything locked into place. One of the key moments was in 1976 when I was listening to Major Ian Thomas at the British Evangelists' Conference near London. As I listened to him, suddenly it was as if the jigsaw puzzle, of which I had lots of pieces, suddenly just fitted itself together into a clear picture of what Christianity is; I wondered why I had never seen it before!

Now, you may have the knowledge, but that still doesn't make you spiritual. Now you need to apply that knowledge, to live it, to allow these truths and principles to be personalized in your life. In other words, just as Jesus fleshed out God, the Christian is to flesh out Jesus. They asked Jesus to show them the Father, and He said, "Anyone who has seen me has seen the Father" (JOHN 14:9). Jesus came to bring God out into the open, and He fleshed him out, lived him out in living color. We have to do the same, so the world might see that Christ lives in us and learn to love Him, too!

We are not in Christianity to get an A+ in theology—did you know that? We are in Christianity to get an A+ in being conformed to the image of Jesus Christ. That is His concern. The spiritual man or the spiritual woman is the one who understands and lives out these truths so that there is no inconsistency between what the Bible says and how he or she is living. Isn't that the battle?

The question is: How do I grow? How do I mature? How can I improve my situation? I give you three essential requirements for spiritual growth and maturation.

We Must Be Saturated in God's Word

To quote Dr. Billy Graham, we must be saturated in God's Word. Paul says, in COLOSSIANS 3:16, "Let the Word of Christ dwell in you richly as you teach and admonish one another with all wisdom, and as you sing psalms, hymns, spiritual songs with gratitude in your hearts to God." Let the Word of Christ dwell in you richly. Paul is not saying to let the Word of Christ *be* in you richly, though I do not doubt for a minute that that is essential. Rather, he says to let the Word of God *dwell* in you richly, that is, be alive in you!

To quote Dr. Billy Graham, we must be saturated in God's Word.

In my home in Scotland there are a few biblical quotations hanging around the house. Let's imagine that we increase these by a hundredfold, so that we have a hundred times more biblical quotes and Scripture verses hanging on the walls. Now our house has got loads of biblical information hanging around it. That is not what makes it a Christian home. What makes it a Christian home is the people living in that house: people living out Christlikeness in relationship to each other. "Let the Word of Christ dwell in you richly." This takes more than just hanging Bible verses all over your mind and all over your brain; it requires that you live them out, allowing them to be alive in you. That is the important act. We can have the truth resident in our minds, but it has to be lived out in our lives, because that is what the word *dwell* means. It means to be alive in you. Let the Word of Christ dwell in you richly, conforming you to the image of the Lord Jesus Christ. You cannot know how to live Christlike unless you read God's Word. You cannot know the promises to claim unless you know the promises made in God's Word. You cannot know God's commands to obey unless you know the commands in God's Word.

Yes, we need to be reading God's Word; it is of prime importance. However, it is one thing to read God's Word, and quite another to make it richly alive in ourselves. In other words, God's Word has to be lived out, fleshed out so that it is a reality in our lives. The biggest problem, as far as Christians are concerned, is the inconsistent

God's Word has to be lived out, fleshed out so that it is a reality in our lives.

reading of God's Word. Over and over again, when people come to me with problems, I ask them if they read the Bible on a regular basis. The answer is so often no. You see, it is almost impossible to be an alive Christian without reading God's word, constantly and consistently. We know that it is impossible to be physically strong without food. That's why most of us eat about three meals a day (plus a few snacks along the way!). Of course you need food, and you need it consistently, and you need good food regularly—but in the end you can take too much and you can take too little. In the same way, you can take too little of God's Word and therefore never grow. There is even a way in which you can take too much of God's Word, if you never let it live in you. Think of some theologians who read and study God's Word every single day: they fill their heads with it, and can recite it to you inside out, yet still not be living Christian lives.

Our need, because we are Christians, is the daily intake of God's Word. If you don't have a regular Bible reading method, let me give you a simple one to start with. Read the book of Proverbs every day. Not the whole book; just read the chapter that is the same as the date. Thirty-one chapters in Proverbs and thirty-one days in the longest months. A chapter a day. We have done this as a family over a number of years. It is one way of getting into the Word on a daily basis. Proverbs is a book of wisdom, so you will be filling your mind with God's wisdom.

Better still is to get a daily Bible reading like Moody Bible Institute's *Today in the Word*. It explains the meaning of the passage chosen for each day. Don't get a system that just has little sayings — there's nothing wrong with little poems and sayings, but these usually are not enough to help you discover what the Bible verse is saying and why it is saying it, which is necessary for the Word to begin to live in your life. We need to be saturated in God's Word.

We Must Be Filled with God's Spirit

The second requirement is that we need to be filled with God's Spirit. Paul says, in Ephesians 5:18, "Do not get drunk on wine, which leads to debauchery. Instead, be filled with the Spirit. Speak to one another with psalms, and hymns and spiritual songs. Sing and make music in your heart to the Lord, always give thanks to God the Father for everything, in the name of our Lord Jesus Christ."

Now, some things are easier to give thanks for than others. My wife has absolutely no problem giving thanks to the Lord for sunshine—none whatsoever. However, I guarantee you that on any morning in Scotland, she will have tremendous difficulty in giving thanks to the Lord for the drizzle, the wind, and the rain. I can tell this because I hear her open the curtains and say, "Not again!" I have asked her if she feels the Lord put her in the wrong climate. She doesn't beat around the bush—"Yes!" We have got to learn to give thanks for *all* things. Isn't it easy to thank the Lord for the good things, for the things that are pleasant? But Paul says to give thanks for everything, and I tell you we can't do that unless we are controlled by God's Spirit. It's totally impossible. There is no way we can do it.

When I take in God's Word, I know what He wants me to say, and how He wants me to live. I want God's Word to be alive in me, a living Word, and that is made possible by the filling of the Holy Spirit.

Who is the Holy Spirit? The Holy Spirit is the third person in the triune Godhead of Father, Son, and Holy Spirit. The Holy Spirit is a person possessing intellect, emotion, and will. When the Holy Spirit comes into the believer's life at the new birth, He comes in completely. Not part of Him. He comes in as He is: a person. You either have the Holy Spirit in your life or you don't. That is the great demarcation line between the believer and the nonbeliever. The nonbeliever does not have the Holy Spirit in his life. The believer does have the Holy Spirit in his life.

Someone has said that a Christian is a person who is in a right relationship to the Lord Jesus by faith, and a spiritual Christian is a person who is in a right relationship to the Holy Spirit by faith. The Holy Spirit has come into the believer's life to fill—to control— his life so that he might live in harmony with the Word of God. It is not that the believer can get more of the Holy Spirit, it is that the Holy Spirit can get more of the believer!

Here's a simple illustration. Take the command in the Bible that says, "Husbands, love your wives." (Don't worry, husbands, I'll get into the next bit in a minute.) It is very difficult to keep that command, and I'll tell you why. When you look at what God means by that command, none of us have an earthly chance. You see, God tells husbands to love their wives as Christ loved the church, and God also defines *love* in 1 CORINTHIANS 13. When you read these together, they come out something like this:

> *A husband's love is patient. (Some of you just blew it on that one there!) A husband's love is kind, it does not envy, it does not boast, it is not proud. A husband's love is not rude, it is not self-seeking, it is not easily angered, it keeps no record of wrongs. A husband's love does not delight in evil but rejoices with the truth. A husband's love always protects, always trusts, always hopes, always perseveres. A husband's love never fails!*

Now, what husband can love his wife like that? I cannot love my wife that way. If you can, I would be delighted if you would tell us all about it! Which of us humans can do this? By ourselves, we can't. That is why Jesus rose from the dead: that by His Spirit, He might come and live within us so that where we are weak He might make us strong. So that He might begin to empower us to live in such a way that He can produce through us the fruit of the Spirit, which is love, joy, peace, patience. That is growth, that is behavior. It is not that this suddenly oozes out of your life, so that your wife says, "Wow, where did that come from?!" No, it is in the situations that demand patience that you and I have to be seeking the Lord's help, because without it we can't be patient and we can't love. When there is the need for peace, we must seek His help, for without Him we cannot bring peace. I don't speak as someone who has arrived but as someone who wants to arrive. When a husband begins to love his wife according to the biblical commands, the Word of God lives, dwells, is alive in his life—and his wife knows it!

So often husbands want to rule the roost. The more you love your wife the way God demands, the more she will submit to your love, because that is what she is longing for. This doesn't mean that one spouse dominates the other; it means that they are both submitting to each other's needs and fulfilling their particular roles. The husband's need is to fulfill his role, to love his wife so that she might become absolutely everything God intended her to be as a wife. As she submits to her husband, she enables him to fulfill his role to the utmost. With each submitting to the other, the end result is that they are like a nut and bolt that join perfectly together, and there is strength in the leadership of the family.

If you separate the nut and bolt, they may be used for various other things, but if they are never used together, they are never used for the purpose for which they were created. The Holy Spirit of God is the one who wants to be the strength in our lives that we might live in harmony with the Word of God.

We Must Be Living by Faith

The final requirement is to live out God's Word in our daily lives—which is the biggest problem for many Christians. I know what the Word says, I know what the Spirit of God promises. How do I do it? It is simple (but not necessarily easy): *by faith*. Here are some verses:

> "The righteous will live by faith"
> (ROMANS 1:17; GALATIANS 3:11).

"Without faith it is impossible to please God"

(HEBREWS 11:6).

These are dominant statements.

How much have you been living by faith today? Do you know the biggest problem I have faced in my Christian life? Coming to God by faith, then trying to live for Him by my efforts, by my works. Each day He wants me to trust Him by faith.

Do you know the biggest problem I have faced in my Christian life? Coming to God by faith ....

Here is a verse from HEBREWS 4. The writer has talked about the children of Israel and how they disobeyed what God said, and that is why they wandered around in the wilderness for forty years. HEBREWS 4:2 says: "For we also have had the gospel preached to us, just as they did: but the message they heard was of no value to them." Do you wonder why it was of no value? Listen. "Because those who heard it did not combine it with faith." They did not combine God's Word, mix it, with faith.

There is a tremendous, compelling need to take the knowledge you have, both of what the Word of God says and of what the Holy Spirit will do, and combine them with faith.

Paul said to the Colossians, in 2:6, "So then, just as you received Christ Jesus as Lord, continue to live in Him." How did they receive Christ Jesus as Lord? By faith. "Rooted and built up in Him, strengthened in the faith as you were taught, overflowing with thankfulness." They had become believers by faith; then they had to continue to live in Him by faith as well. Faith is always the requirement that God demands of us, for without faith it is impossible to please Him!

Many years ago, I preached in Bethany Beach Tabernacle in Michigan. I was unaware that I had been saying, over and over again, while I was preaching, "God is saying, 'Trust me, trust me, just trust me.'" Apparently, I said it constantly, according to a young man in the pews that day. I didn't know I was saying it over and over again, and maybe I wasn't saying it as often as this person thought, but this young man who was listening thought that was *all* I said all night! Well, God *is* saying, "Just trust me, just trust me." Later I met with that young man and his wife. The end result was that he went to Bethel Seminary and for many years ran a ministry in Hawaii. (So you had better trust Him if you want to get to Hawaii!) As we talked together, we discovered that his problem was that he knew what God wanted him to do, and he knew what he wanted to do; however, this young couple found that the most difficult thing was to trust God, put their faith in God, and allow God to do as He wished in their lives.

So often we are hesitant to trust God, to put our confidence in His promises, in His provision, in His power—and yet He is always saying, "Trust me." All of us can say that when we have truly trusted Him, not once has He let us down. Most of us can say that we have let Him down many times, but God never lets us down. We must mix our knowledge of His Word with faith for it to become a reality in our lives. Then we will say, like the apostle Paul in GALATIANS 2:20, "I have been crucified with Christ. I no longer live, but Christ lives in me. The life I live in the body, I live by faith in the Son of God, who loved me and gave himself for me."

Let me give you a simple illustration of trust. You are walking across open land and you come to a ravine. It is 100 feet down. It is 100 feet across. There is a raging torrent 100 feet down at the bottom of the ravine. You look up the ravine, as far as the eye can see, and there is no bridge. You look all the way down, and there is no bridge. The only bridge is the one right there in front of you. It is three feet wide, it has no railings along the sides of it, and it swings in the wind. There is a sign that says, "This bridge is guaranteed to break if 50 lbs. or more is placed on it." Let me ask you, how much faith do you need to get across this bridge? It does not matter how much faith you have, you will not get across that bridge. The important fact is not your faith, it is the truth concerning the bridge. If the truth is that it will break if 50 pounds or more is put on it, it doesn't matter how much you put your faith in the bridge, it will break and you will not get across.

Now suppose that the sign says, "This bridge is guaranteed to hold 5,000 lbs." Let me ask you, how much faith do you need to get across? You know something. You only need enough faith to shuffle one foot in front of the other. You can be saying, "Oh, Mother, I hate heights, oh, oh, I hate it," and you can go on like that all the way across — but you will get to the other side, the same as the person who is not afraid of heights, who couldn't care less that there are no railings, and who runs across and has the audacity to turn round halfway, as he is still running, and shout, "Come on, it's OK!" You will get to the other side even if you just shuffle one foot in front of the other, because you are trusting, putting your faith in the bridge to do what it was created to do: hold you and get you across to the other side.

That is why Jesus said, in MATTHEW 17:20, "If you have faith as small as a mustard seed," that is all you need. Day by day we come to the commands of God. He asks us to put our trust in Him. Sometimes we put our trust in His commands even though we are kicking and screaming and saying we don't want to go this way. Isn't that true?

Then there are the promises of God. Some people like to worry rather than trust. (They are usually melancholics.) There is the problem. Why trust when you can worry! But God gives us promises and we are asked to trust them, step on them, rely on them. There have been times in my life and in our marriage when all we had to hang onto were the promises of God. We had absolutely nothing else, but we found those promises more than adequate!

Some years ago, I was going out to the States for four weeks, and when that trip was over two U.S. couples were coming to stay with us. The day before I left for the United States, my wife asked me to do some work on the shower before our guests arrived. I am one of many husbands who usually have chores to do and don't get around to them. On that day, I started to work on the shower and discovered that we had a problem with the outside wall of our house, which had only been up seven years. We had what is known as wet rot, and we also discovered that we had dry rot. (If you know anything about dry rot, you know we had big problems.) The company that deals with such problems came in and told us we needed approximately $8,000 worth of repair work. I had to leave my wife with this when I departed for the United States. I cried almost nonstop for two days. I could not stop crying.

I found myself kneeling and telling God that I only have $100 in the bank. No one else would take responsibility: insurance wouldn't touch it, the builder wouldn't take responsibility. This was one of the times we were left with nothing but the promise of God. Isn't it terrible to say that is *all* we were left with? That was all we needed! The repair company phoned me in Pittsburgh to tell me good and bad news. The bad news was that it was going to cost another $5,000; the good news was that we'd caught it early—otherwise, the damage would have been right through the rafters and ruined the whole house within six months. That was the good news!

So we were left with God's promises. I say this carefully. Every single bill was paid. Money came from places I could not imagine, including an insurance company that changed its decision, and in the end we were able to give away money because excess money came in and there was no way we were going to hold onto it. We were able to give $2,500 each to three children whose fathers had been killed on the mission field. So, from having nothing, the whole bill was paid and three kids were helped. All from claiming the promises of God: "Cast your anxiety on him for he cares for you" (1 PETER 5:7). "We know that in all things God works for the good of those who love him." What we discovered was that all we need are the promises of God; all we need are the commands of God; all we need is the power of God. But the only way this can be activated is to put our trust in that provision, in that promise, in that command, and mix it with faith and then let God do His work. When that happens, it is nothing short of astounding.

6 RESPONSE, APPLICATION, AND CONCLUSION

In conclusion, a summary. Adam, created in the image of God, filled by the Spirit of God, and living by faith in obedience to the Word of God, reflected the truth about God. Jesus Christ, the second Adam, filled by the Spirit of God, living by faith in obedience to the Word of God, reflected the truth about God.

He who has seen me has seen the Father. As the Father sent me, so send I you. The believer, the new creation, filled by the Spirit of God and living by faith in obedience to the Word of God, reflects the truth about God. We call it Christlikeness, we call it the fruit of the Spirit, we call it godliness. What it means is that once more man is back in the relationship that he had in the beginning, that he lost and had restored. He is reconciled to God, restored to function and right reflection of God's likeness.

The Bad News Is That You Are Separated from God

How do you need to apply what you have read?

Information without application can produce desperation. However, information with application will produce transformation.

Where are you on your spiritual journey? You may say, "I am not on a spiritual journey." That is where you are on your spiritual journey: you are not on it! Nevertheless, you are probably searching and don't realize it. Around the world, all humans ask the same three questions in various ways:

1. Where have I come from?
2. What am I doing here?
3. Where am I going?

That is probably where you are on your spiritual journey. You are at the searching stage.

You may be facing the wrong way as far as Jesus is concerned. I hope I have helped you to turn around and face the right way, even if you are a hundred miles away. Some of you may be ninety miles away. I hope you moved up ten miles to eighty miles, and some from eighty to seventy, and some from seventy to sixty, and so on. In the end, however, you are either a believer in the Lord Jesus Christ as your Savior or you are a nonbeliever. There are no in-betweens. You are either dead in Adam or you are alive in Jesus. You are either walking in the light or you are walking in the darkness. You are either standing on the rock or you are sinking in the sand. You are either on the narrow road that leads to life or you are on the broad road that leads to destruction. It is one or the other.

If you are a nonbeliever, you need to trust in the Lord Jesus Christ as your Savior and cross over from death to life and be saved, rescued, delivered, liberated! The facts are simple and I hope they have become obvious to you.

You Are a Sinner

- You have fallen short of the glory of God.

- You have missed the mark and broken God's commandments.

- You are not as bad as you could be, but you are not as good
as you should be.

- Your life is like a car with no gas in the tank. Your life has
a God-shaped vacuum in it that only God can fill.

Jesus Died for Your Sin

The good news is that Jesus took your place. "For God so loved
the world that he gave his one and only Son, that whoever believes
in him shall not perish but have eternal life" (John 3:16). "You see,
at just the right time, when we were still powerless, Christ died for
the ungodly" (ROMANS 5:6).

- Jesus paid your price. "We see Jesus, who was made a little
lower than the angels, crowned with glory and honor because he suffered death, so that by the grace of God he
might taste death for everyone" (HEBREWS 2:9).

- Jesus satisfied God's justice for your sin. "He is the atoning
sacrifice for our sins, and not only for ours but also for the
sins of the whole world" (1 JOHN 2:2).

- Jesus made a way back to God for you. "God was reconciling the world to himself in Christ, not counting men's sins
against them" (2 CORINTHIANS 5:19).

Everything that needed to be done has been done, and now God offers you salvation as a free gift that can be received only by faith.

The Necessity of Faith

Jesus' death on the cross was essential for God's justice to be satisfied. "He did it to demonstrate his justice at the present time, so as to be just and the one who justifies those who have faith in Jesus" (ROMANS 3:26). Jesus' death was acceptable to God not because of who Jesus was, but because of what He was: "a lamb without blemish or defect" (1 PETER 1:19). Christ became the ground on which God can "be just and the one who justifies those who have faith in Jesus."

Objectively, Jesus is the Savior of all men and women—but subjectively, only those who believe are saved. Potentially, Jesus is the Savior of all men and women—but effectively, only those who believe experience salvation. The Biblical truth of "a ransom for all men and women" brings worship, adoration, and praise to God, who is rich in mercy, great in love, and abundant in grace; He is not willing that any should perish, but desires that all should come to a knowledge of the truth.

The question has never changed over the centuries. It remains the same today: "What must I do to be saved?" The answer has remained constant as well: "Believe in the Lord Jesus Christ, and you will be saved" (ACTS 16:30–31).

Jesus gives an interesting reply in JOHN 6:28–29: "Then they asked him, 'What must we do to do the works God requires?' Jesus answered, 'The work of God is this: to believe in the one he has sent.'"

ROMANS 4:4–5 says, "Now when a man works, his wages are not credited to him as a gift, but as an obligation. However, to the man who does not work but trusts God who justifies the wicked, his faith is credited as righteousness." There are three elements involved in a "step" faith. These are not separate steps but intertwined truths. When a step of faith takes place, there is knowledge of sin, acknowledgment of Jesus as Savior, and faith as the requirement fed to the intellect. Conviction of these truths with assent is experienced through the emotion, and trust in that information is expressed by the will. To have faith is to believe in or to trust in Christ for salvation.

Faith must have an object. Faith is faith, whether I sit on a chair or believe in Christ. Faith is simply trusting. A person who believes in Buddha and a person who believes in Christ both believe, but only one is saved. The difference is the object of their faith.

The decision is yours: to believe in Jesus as your Savior or not to believe in Him; to trust in Jesus as your Savior or not to trust in Him; to accept Jesus as your Savior or not to accept Him.

Let me ask you two questions:

1. Do you see any reason why you should not trust in Jesus as your Savior? If you see no reason why you shouldn't believe in Jesus, then

2. Are you willing to put your trust in Him now as your Savior? If your answer is yes, let me invite you to pray this prayer of trust to Him now.

Lord Jesus, I am a sinner. Thank you for dying for my sin. Thank you for rising from the dead to give me life. I turn from my sin to you. I put my trust in you. I invite you into my life to be my Savior. Thank you for coming in.

The Sad News Is That You Are a Carnal Christian

You may be a believer, but for various reasons find that your life is more defeat than victory. Spiritual growth has been slow. It has been a battle and you feel like giving up. You have tried to live for Jesus but have failed.

That is both the point and the problem. You have been trying to live for Jesus—when He rose from the dead to live for you! You see, there are believers who have Jesus living in them by His Spirit but who have never allowed Him to live in them and through them. They came to Jesus by faith and then tried to live for Him by their own works and efforts. As Paul wrote to the Colossians: "So then, just as you received Christ Jesus as Lord, continue to live in Him, rooted and built up in Him, strengthened in the faith as you were taught, and overflowing with thankfulness" (COLOSSIANS 2:6). To the Romans he said, "The righteous will live by faith" (ROMANS 1:17).

These believers have a life they have never lived. They have gas in the tank but are still pushing the car! Carnal Christianity arises out of various errors and attitudes, but can be resolved by honest confession. Lord, I can't; you can! Lord, I won't, but you will. Lord, I make myself available to you for all you have made yourself available to me!

The Carnal Believer Is Not Abiding in Christ

JOHN 15:1–17:

> [1] I am the true vine, and my Father is the gardener.
> [2] He cuts off every branch in me that bears no fruit, while every branch that does bear fruit he prunes so that it will be even more fruitful.

³ You are already clean because of the word I have spoken to you.

⁴ Remain in me, and I will remain in you. No branch can bear fruit by itself; it must remain in the vine. Neither can you bear fruit unless you remain in me.

⁵ I am the vine; you are the branches. If a man remains in me and I in him, he will bear much fruit; apart from me you can do nothing.

⁶ If anyone does not remain in me, he is like a branch that is thrown away and withers; such branches are picked up, thrown into the fire and burned.

⁷ If you remain in me and my words remain in you, ask whatever you wish, and it will be given you.

⁸ This is to my Father's glory, that you bear much fruit, showing yourselves to be my disciples.

⁹ As the Father has loved me, so have I loved you. Now remain in my love.

¹⁰ If you obey my commands, you will remain in my love, just as I have obeyed my Father's commands and remain in his love.

¹¹ I have told you this so that my joy may be in you and that your joy may be complete.

¹² My command is this: Love each other as I have loved you.

¹³ Greater love has no one than this, that he lay down his life for his friends.

¹⁴ You are my friends if you do what I command.

¹⁵ I no longer call you servants, because a servant does not know his master's business. Instead, I have called you friends, for everything that I learned from my Father I have made known to you.

¹⁶ You did not choose me, but I chose you and appointed you to go and bear fruit—fruit that will last. Then the Father will give you whatever you ask in my name.

¹⁷ This is my command: Love each other.

The key statements from John 15 are:

⁵ I am the vine; you are the branches. If a man remains in me and I in him, he will bear much fruit; apart from me you can do nothing.

⁷ If you remain in me and my words remain in you, ask whatever you wish, and it will be given you.

¹¹ I have told you this so that my joy may be in you and that your joy may be complete.

God wants believers' lives to be fruitful, their prayers to be answered, and their joy to be complete! However, it depends on believers remaining in Jesus; that is, being alive in our relationship with Christ by faith. This necessitates reading His word each day, so that we may know the commands to obey, the promises to claim, and the truth that sets us free! It necessitates praying each day about everything and making ourselves available to him as living sacrifices.

Lord, here is my mind to think through, my emotion to feel through, my will to decide through, and my body to live through. Lord, here I am; use me today.

The Carnal Believer Is Not Walking in the Spirit

Galatians 5:16–26:

16 So I say, live by the Spirit, and you will not gratify the desires of the sinful nature.

17 For the sinful nature desires what is contrary to the Spirit, and the Spirit what is contrary to the sinful nature. They are in conflict with each other, so that you do not do what you want.

18 But if you are led by the Spirit, you are not under law.

19 The acts of the sinful nature are obvious: sexual immorality, impurity and debauchery;

20 idolatry and witchcraft; hatred, discord, jealousy, fits of rage, selfish ambition, dissensions, factions

21 and envy; drunkenness, orgies, and the like. I warn you, as I did before, that those who live like this will not inherit the kingdom of God.

22 But the fruit of the Spirit is love, joy, peace, patience, kindness, goodness, faithfulness,

23 gentleness and self-control. Against such things there is no law.

24 Those who belong to Christ Jesus have crucified the sinful nature with its passions and desires.

25 Since we live by the Spirit, let us keep in step with the Spirit.

26 Let us not become conceited, provoking and envying each other.

The key statements from Galatians 5 are:

[16] "So I say, live by the Spirit, and you will not gratify the desires of the sinful nature."

You always overcome the negative with the positive, darkness with light, error with truth, and the desires of a sinful nature by living in the Spirit. Too many believers spend their time trying not to be negative, but that does not produce positive behavior. They spend their time fighting the darkness, but that doesn't produce light. They spend their time fighting error, but that doesn't produce truth. They spend their time fighting the desires of the sinful nature, but that doesn't produce living by the Spirit. They put the cart before the horse because they are not in fact living by faith!

[18] "But if you are led by the Spirit, you are not under law."

This does *not* mean that the believer is lawless. Believers must be lawful, but they keep the law from a whole different perspective. Earlier in this chapter, Paul says, in verse 14, "The entire law is summed up in a single command: 'Love your neighbor as yourself.'" Read carefully! When believers are living by the Spirit, they are abiding in Christ and they are being controlled by the Spirit. The result is that the fruit of the Spirit is produced in their lives—and the fruit of the Spirit is love. Now, if you love your neighbor, you will not lie to your neighbor, so you automatically keep the law without even thinking about it! If you love your neighbor, you will not steal from your neighbor, so you automatically keep the law without even thinking about it! If you love your neighbor, you will not commit adultery with your neighbor's wife or husband, so you automatically keep the law without even thinking about it! The positive is handling the negative, the light is dispelling the darkness, the truth is overcoming the error, and living by the Spirit is overcoming the desires of the sinful nature! You are spiritual, not carnal.

> [25] "Since we live by the Spirit, let us keep in step with the Spirit."

Since we can live the Christian life only by the power of the Lord Jesus living in us by the Spirit, every day we must be keeping in step with the Holy Spirit, as revealed in the Word of God and the leading of the Spirit.

God wants believers' lives to be controlled by the Spirit, so that the fruit of the Spirit is produced in their lives and conforms them to the likeness of Jesus. This necessitates reading God's Word daily so that we know His commands to obey, His promises to claim, and His truth that sets us free; it necessitates praying each day about everything and making ourselves available to him as living sacrifices.

> *Lord, here is my mind; control it by your Spirit that I might think your thoughts. Lord, here is my emotion; control it by your Spirit so that I feel your feelings. Lord, here is my will; control it by your Spirit so that I might make your decisions. Lord, here is my body; control it by your Spirit so that I might live your life to the people I come in contact with today.*

The Good News Is That You Are a Spiritual Christian!

What a joy it is to know that, even though you have not arrived, you are traveling with Jesus down the right road and in the right direction! Your relationship with Him is being strengthened by faith and being conformed to His likeness. What a joy to know that "he who began a good work in you will carry it on to completion until the day of Christ Jesus" (PHILIPPIANS 1:6), when "we shall be like him, for we shall see him as he is" (1 JOHN 3:2).

You Are Abiding in Christ

You have learned quickly or slowly, through joy and through sadness, that abiding in Christ is the only way that fruit can be produced through your life. You have discovered that you cannot produce God through your life—only God can do that! This has caused you to pray daily to Him as the source who meets all your needs, and you have discovered that He is at work in your life. Your joy is complete! Don't let anyone try to downgrade or tarnish your experience, because you can experience complete joy even in the darkest storm; joy that you are reconciled to God, joy that you are regenerated by the Holy Spirit, and joy that you are being conformed to His likeness. God has no plan to destroy you. His plan is to complete you to your potential and gifting. In the darkest times, this is the complete joy that can come only from its source in a Father God who loves you with an everlasting love.

You Are Living by the Spirit

You have learned quickly or slowly, through joy and through sadness, that to live by the Spirit is the only way to overcome the desires of the flesh. You have discovered that you cannot overcome the desires of the flesh—only God can do that! This happened at the cross when Jesus defeated the devil.

The devil, now a defeated foe, has no rights, no authority, and no power over the believer who has moved from the kingdom of darkness to the kingdom of light, from dead in Adam to alive in Jesus. The devil can lie, tempt, and seek to deceive the believer. Now you are in truth struggles as the devil seeks to lie, tempt, and deceive you, but you have discovered that the truth sets you free! As a believer, you are not in a power struggle: that took place at the cross and Jesus was victorious. Now, as a believer, you are in Christ and all that he accomplished at the cross and by the resurrection is true for you, too.

You are in a truth struggle with the devil, the father of lies, whether to believe his lie or God's truth! You have discovered that the law was never given for believers, but for sinners, to reveal sin and be the schoolmaster to bring them to Christ. You have discovered that the law is the mirror that reveals sin, but it is not the soap that cleanses away sin! You have discovered that you are on the side that has already won, not the side that is winning! You have discovered that you live, but that it is not you: it is Jesus living in you, and when you live the life in the body, you live by faith in the Son of God who loved you and gave himself for you.

Therefore, day by day your desire is to keep in step with the Spirit: to be available as a living sacrifice; to experience godliness with contentment as great gain; to be a pauper but the child of the King; to have nothing but experience everything—and you know that where your heart is, there your treasure will be also.

You are still discovering that you are accountable to God for all that you have. You are learning that you will be judged, on His terms only, for your stewardship of all that He has given you: money, talent, time, and gifting. You are seeing the world and your life through His eyes and hearing the cries of others through His ears.

Be aware that never will the devil lie to you, deceive you, or tempt you more than in the area of money and material possessions.

He will give you every argument—from politics, education, humanism, democracy, and "common sense"—to indulge your flesh. Lose here and you lose! Win here and you win! Jesus put it this way: "Do not store up for yourselves treasures on earth, where moth and rust destroy, and where thieves break in and steal. But store up for yourselves treasures in heaven, where moth and rust do not destroy, and where thieves do not break in and steal" (MATTHEW 6:19–20).

"Praise be to the God and Father of our Lord Jesus Christ! In his great mercy he has given us new birth into a living hope through the resurrection of Jesus Christ from the dead, and into an inheritance that can never perish, spoil or fade—kept in heaven for you, who through faith are shielded by God's power until the coming of the salvation that is ready to be revealed in the last time. In this you greatly rejoice, though now for a little while you may have had to suffer grief in all kinds of trials. These have come so that your faith—of greater worth than gold, which perishes even though refined by fire—may be proved genuine and may result in praise, glory and honor when Jesus Christ is revealed. Though you have not seen him, you love him; and even though you do not see him now, you believe in him and are filled with an inexpressible and glorious joy, for you are receiving the goal of your faith, the salvation of your souls" (1 PETER 1:3–9).

Appendix 1—About the Heralds Trust

Back in the late 1950s, a group of young Christians began experimenting with the hymns and worship songs of the day, making them more upbeat and interesting to their peers. It soon became clear that the interest in their music was bringing with it an interest in the message behind the music.

After a few years, the band, by now named "The Heralds," was playing around Scotland and were invited to play on a BBC television show called "Epilogue." This exposure made them well-known in Scotland's Christian community, and more bookings rolled in. During it all, the group kept the Christian message well to the forefront of their activities.

From 1963 on, The Heralds began to be involved in large-scale outreach events, playing to packed halls around the country. The response to these events was overwhelming, with many people committing themselves to Jesus. In 1966, however, Ian Leitch, one of The Heralds' vocalists, followed God's call into further service. He and his wife, Morag, left to study at the Moody Bible Institute in Chicago.

Meanwhile, The Heralds decided to carry on, though finding that greater success required more and more time and effort. Eventually, the Heralds realized that they required a full-time worker. So it was that, in 1969, Ian and Morag Leitch returned to the fold to spearhead The Heralds' dynamic Christian outreach. To put things on a proper footing, it was decided to turn The Heralds into a charitable trust: The Heralds Trust.

The ministry of the Heralds Trust has gone from strength to strength. As well as working in outreach with churches, the Trust aims to teach and train the next generation of young evangelists to carry God's word to an increasingly needy world. Ian Leitch remains the spearhead of these activities, having been an employee of the Trust since day one.

Ian Leitch has developed New Life seminars to put doctrine into application. Each One Bring One events take place in a non-threatening environment where Ian, or another evangelist from the Heralds Trust, presents a straightforward gospel message and invites commitment at the end of the gathering. Ian has also created Prepare 2 Share seminars, which offer three levels of training that equip participants to share their Christian faith in an exciting and relevant way. Students are grounded in the basics of the Christian faith and taught how to communicate the message to others.

The principal objectives of The Heralds Trust are the proclamation of the Christian gospel, and the teaching, training, and encouraging of local Christian churches both in Britain and abroad. The Heralds Trust offers these seminars:

New Life

Each One Bring One

Prepare 2 Share

For more information about these events, or to schedule a speaking engagement with Ian Leitch, please visit The Heralds Trust Web site at: http://www.theheraldstrust.org/

theheraldstrust

Appendix 2 — Recommended Books

George, Bob. (1989). *Classic Christianity.* Eugene, OR: Harvest House.

Price, Charles W. (1995). *Christ for Real.* Grand Rapids, MI: Kregel Publications.

Thomas, Major Ian. (1974). *Mystery of Godliness.* Grand Rapids, MI: Zondervan.

Thomas, Major Ian. (1989). *The Saving Life of Christ.* Grand Rapids, MI: Zondervan.

Appendix 3—Illustrations

Right Relationship, Right Behavior

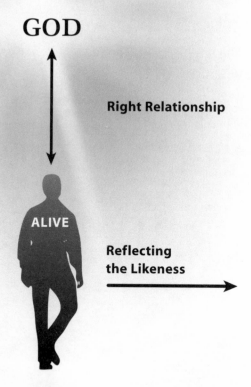

Then God said, "Let us make man in our image, in our likeness."
So God created man in his own image.

—Genesis 1:26a, 27a

Wrong Relationship, Wrong Behavior

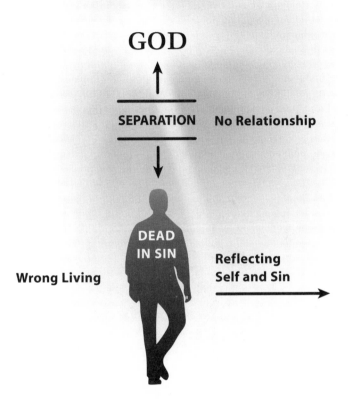

The wages of sin is death.

—Romans 6:23a

All have sinned and fall short of the glory of God.

—Romans 3:23a

The Cross, the Resurrection

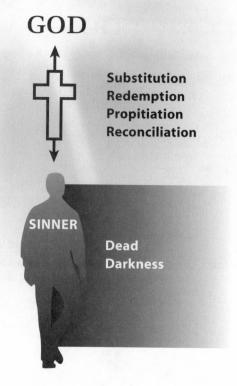

GOD

Substitution
Redemption
Propitiation
Reconciliation

SINNER

Dead
Darkness

For the son of Man came to seek and to save what was lost.

—Luke 19:10

I have come that they may have life and have it to the full.

—John 10:10b

Restored Relationship, Restored Behavior

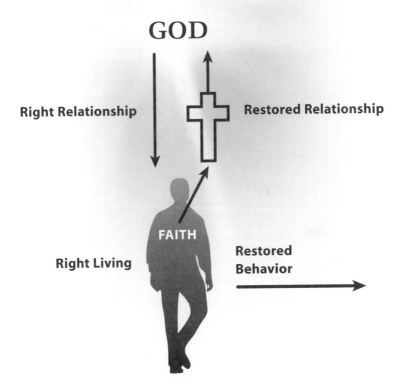

When we were God's enemies, we were reconciled to him through the death of his Son, how much more, having been reconciled, shall we be saved through his life!

—ROMANS 5:10

Grace Acres Press

Grace Acres Press products and services bring joy to your heart and life. Visit us at www.GraceAcresPress.com.

Other titles available from Grace Acres Press:

Beyond the Compass:
Learning to See the Unseen
by DAVE WAGER
Foreword by Dave Abbatacola
$11.95
See what you have never seen in your spiritual journey with this 21-day guided journal.

Strengthened by Grace: A Systematic
Theology Handbook
by RICHARD E. WAGER
Foreword by Art Rorheim
$19.95
Easy-to-use theology reference for your home. Prepares you to give reasons and rationale for your beliefs.

For orders or information about quantity discounts or reprints,
> Call 888-700-GRACE (4722)
> Fax (303) 681-9996
> Email info@GraceAcresPress.com